PETER LORIMER

PETER LORIMER
Leeds And Scotland Hero

Peter Lorimer and Phil Rostron

Best Wishes
Birger Eriksen.

MAINSTREAM
PUBLISHING

EDINBURGH AND LONDON

First published in Great Britain in 2002 by
MAINSTREAM PUBLISHING (EDINBURGH) LTD
7 Albany Street
Edinburgh EH1 3UG

ISBN 1 84018 612 7

A catalogue record for this book is available from the British Library

Typeset in Berkeley and Trade Gothic

Printed in Great Britain by
Creative Print & Design Wales, Ebbw Vale

Best Wishes
Maureen.

contents

dedication

For my mother, Janet, whose lifelong sacrifice, support
and help are much appreciated.

acknowledgements

MY THANKS GO TO PHIL ROSTRON, SPORTS EDITOR OF THE *YORKSHIRE EVENING Post*, for putting my life into words; three members of the YEP staff, David Helliwell, Stuart Martel and Paul Dews, for their painstaking revision; and the photographers who, over the years, have donated their work to my private collection, from which the photographic section has been assembled.

foreword

BY TOMMY DOCHERTY

ONE OF THE GREATEST INJUSTICES IN FOOTBALL HISTORY IS THAT PETER Lorimer should win the miserly total of 21 international caps for Scotland. He was deprived of a clutch of honours by getting caught up in the politically sensitive area of the apartheid laws affecting South Africa at a time when double standards were being applied: while it was acceptable for Springbok cricketers and runners to perform in Britain, the same principle was not attached to British sportsmen going the other way.

The swingeing life ban imposed upon Peter by the Scottish Football Association was a knee-jerk reaction to a ripple of criticism. Not only was it excessive in the extreme, it was also as glaring a case of self-denial as is possible to imagine.

When I was appointed manager of Scotland in succession to Bobby Brown in 1972 the challenge facing me was to qualify for the 1974 World Cup in West Germany. In order to achieve this I needed all the best Scottish players available for selection. You don't go to war with half an army, and it was with this at the forefront of my mind that I implored the SFA to lift their ban with immediate effect.

The prospect facing me was that I would have to achieve a difficult goal without the greatest player in the world, because in my view that was what Peter Lorimer was. I determined that the rock-solid foundation for my squad would be honed from Leeds United, who were gracing English football with one of the finest teams ever assembled. Driven by Billy Bremner, they boasted on the left wing the elegant and tricky Eddie Gray, who was so light on his feet that he could run a mile in the snow and not leave a footprint, and on the right the forceful Lorimer, who delivered crosses with deadly accuracy and possessed a shot so powerful that it would shatter granite.

I had followed Peter's career closely since he was a boy. Just about the worst-kept secret in football when he was growing up was that there was a certain Son of Dundee who would one day explode onto the scene and make a lasting impression, and when I embarked upon my managerial career at Chelsea in the early 1960s I was desperate to sign him. I have never known so many football club representatives in attendance at a match as when Peter played for Scotland Schoolboys against England at Hampden and here, in a single performance, he took their collective breath away with a demonstration of why he was such hot property.

That he chose Leeds United ahead of a host of envious clubs was the Yorkshire club's good fortune and their rivals' bad luck. His goalscoring prowess and his role as the provider of goals played a huge part in the phenomenal run of success enjoyed by Leeds under Don Revie and he left an indelible imprint upon the club's history as well as that of Scottish international football.

It was fortuitous timing on my part to have left Chelsea in 1967 just before they faced Leeds at Elland Road. Having warmed up four days earlier with a 9–0 defeat of the part-timers of Spora Luxembourg in the Fairs Cup, with Lorimer belting in four of them, they proceeded to take Chelsea apart and raced to a 7–0 drubbing with Lash again on the scoresheet.

Peter is a nice man, intelligent, unassuming and understated, and I am privileged and honoured to make this contribution to what is a stunning autobiography. As you will discover, I know that Peter, a players' player, holds the same sentiments as those reflected in one of my favourite observations as I tour the after-dinner speaking circuit: the ideal football club board comprises three men – two dead and one dying.

chapter one

THE FERRYMAN

THAT I WAS AMONG THE HUNDREDS OF THOUSANDS WHO ENTERED THE WORLD in the post-war baby boom may explain why my life has been littered with battles, some for which I have had a great appetite and others of a personal nature which, really, have been of my own engineering. My father Peter was a seafarer whose duties with the Royal Navy meant that he was a rare visitor to the home in Church Street, Broughty Ferry, which he had set up with my mother, Janet. They had met when he was home on leave, she having moved from her native Fife to engage in nursing at the local hospital.

Chez Lorimer was upstairs, first floor, in a terraced row. Basically, it had just one bedroom, in which mum and dad slept, while I shared a corner of the lounge with my brother, Joe, who is five years older than me. We slept in the one bed in this corner of the room with a curtain pulled across to serve as a partition. They were spartan conditions, with the old tin bath in use when it was family bathtime and only an outside toilet. All the fathers had just come back from the war and inevitably there was the highest population explosion in history.

Broughty Ferry in the war was a little fishing village which had once enjoyed the reputation of being the richest square mile in Europe, being the chosen home for the jute barons of Dundee. By the time I was born, on 14 December 1964, the barons had gone, but to this day it is still regarded as affluent and posh. It overlooks the entrance to the Firth of Tay, which was a strategic location in the days of naval conflict. Its castle dates from the fifteenth century. By 1855, when the Crimean War was in progress, it was a ruin and was purchased by the government and restored to protect the Tay from Russian warships. The nautical heritage of the place is reflected in all the local hostelries and I well remember that in 1959 the Broughty Ferry lifeboat *Mona* was called to action and was lost with all hands.

When I was young the place had a real holiday feel about it. There were ice-cream parlours all down the front and people didn't go to England or abroad for their holidays, they went to Broughty Ferry. Dundee people went there like Yorkshire folk go to Bridlington and Lancastrians to Blackpool. We didn't like that. It was an intrusion into our privacy. We used to call them 'orrey' people, meaning rough, city dwellers. They were in our space – on the sands where we liked to fish and in the parks where we liked to play football.

I attended Eastern School and by the age of seven I was playing football for the Under-12 team. When I went to the big school, I was playing for the Under-15s at the age of 12. It was obvious to a lot of people that I had been blessed with ability, and whereas individuals can deteriorate or level off, or go off football altogether as the years go by, I never thought about how great it would be to be a footballer, just about how far I would go in the game once I got into it.

I lived for football as a kid. If it was raining and we had a night match I would spend every minute thinking 'Oh no, I hope they don't call the match off'. Every night we would play in the street until our mothers called us in. There were not the distractions of the modern world such as television and computers. You made your own entertainment. In summer we would transfer our football to the park. At first there would be 10 of you, then 20, then 30 and then 40; so many that you would have to split into two games. Recently I returned to that park with the intention of watching the kids play football while I walked the dog. There wasn't a youngster in sight.

That is why Britain is no longer producing the players that we used to produce. This is especially true of Scotland. Every team was once littered with Scottish players – particularly Leeds and Liverpool down the years – and on one memorable occasion, against Ipswich, Leeds fielded an all-Scottish team.

I used to go to bed on a Friday night fully kitted up in the tangerine colours of Eastern for the next day's football in case my mother was late in shouting me or the alarm clock failed to go off. Sometimes I would play up front and at others at centre-half, because anywhere over the halfway line against these titchy keepers I would score goals. I was probably better off further back because I used to hit the ball so hard that, from a distance, the ball would at least be coming down as it reached the goal. I would score eight or ten goals every game. When I was 12, my father made the mistake of putting me on threepence a goal, and after three or four weeks that had to be stopped because it was taking more than a few pints out of his pocket! His reasoning, or excuse, was that I was already receiving ten shillings a week from Leeds United and that was more than enough to keep a boy of my age happy. By now I was playing two games a day: in the morning for my school and in the afternoon for Broughty YMCA. I would go home after the first of them and my mother would have fresh kit ready while I gulped my dinner down with the mud from the match still clinging to my legs, face and hair. Then it was straight off to the afternoon game and my day was not complete unless I had scored 12 or 14 goals aggregate in the two matches.

I was the talk of Broughty Ferry. The pros from Dundee, like the left back Bobby Cox (who once played for Scotland), would go round looking at the school games on a Saturday morning, earmarking kids for the future. He gave me a big report and while the locals couldn't know that in their midst was someone who would play for the greatest Leeds United side of them all, and in a World Cup for Scotland, they were aware of someone who might go places. In those days 'B' internationals were played in the afternoons – there were no floodlights – and I nicked off school one day to attend my first match.

Scotland were playing England at Dundee and the trick was to get an adult going through the turnstile to push you underneath it and into the ground. 'Can you get us in, mister?' you would ask. Of course, you dared not tell your parents that you were skipping school to watch football.

Scottish football matches attracted huge crowds in those days. There was little else to do and nowhere else to go. There would be up to 40,000 even at places like Dundee.

I had an uncle called Paddy who had been a very good amateur footballer, and his treat at the back end of the summer school holiday was to take me to watch the great Hibs team. I would go on the train from Cowdenbeath to Edinburgh, over the bridge, to watch the Hibernian Famous Five – Smith, Johnstone, Reilly, Turnbull and Ormond – little knowing then that I was going to play in the World Cup for Scotland with Willie Ormond as my team manager. Further, Eddie Turnbull was to be my Scotland manager at Under-23 level.

I was saddened to hear of the death last year of Bobby Johnstone. He was known as a drinker – he had a real drinker's nose and was quite tubby. Thinking of him reminds me that in those days being a professional footballer was nothing like it is now. Training amounted to ten laps of the pitch but, let's be fair, most players were working men and only part-time footballers. They would be down the pit, only coming up to play a match. And being a footballer was not generally looked upon as anything special; just a means of earning a bit more money. In fact, you were looked down upon. I remember when I first started playing being asked on holiday by someone with a bit of money what I did in life and when I said that I was a footballer the look he gave me said: 'How common. Yes, but what do you do?' Realistically, when you looked at the wages, you could see where he was coming from, but to you it was a big thing.

We had a big family. My father was one of six, so there were plenty of aunts, uncles and cousins around. I had a wonderful childhood. I never wanted for anything. There was always good food, like the sumptuous local fish and chips, and bread and butter piled high with jam which finished up all over your face. We lived next door to the Regal cinema. Our wall went right up to the cinema and, after first seeing all the films, we were able to keep track of the storyline on a nightly basis by the musical accompaniment. Every dramatic moment, like the approach of the cavalry or the Indians, was heightened by the urgency and the volume of the music and in the house we'd be playing the parts as the films progressed. Because of the noise from the cinema we couldn't get to sleep until after half past ten.

We were one of the first families in our street to acquire a television and this was prompted by the Coronation in 1952. Football internationals were played on Wednesday afternoons then and, of course, it would be a case of waking up on the morning of these matches and saying: 'Mum, I feel ill.' She knew the real agenda and, despite making token noises of admonishment, she would let me stay off to watch the action. The street was a community – doors were never locked – and because we had a television set our house was overflowing with people who wanted to see the football. Nobody fell out with you that week! And even if they did, the football was the peacemaker. I well remember that the programme broadcast just before the football was *Bill and Ben*, so it was a full afternoon's entertainment for the kids.

My only interest in life other than football was fishing in the River Tay. We knew the movement of the tide and would gear our days around it. When the tide was out at, say, midday, we would play football until then and spend the rest of the day digging sandworm bait until it was time to go back and play football again. We would do this for two days, so that we would have sufficient bait for a decent fishing session. Fishing and football. Football and fishing. Joe went off to a more academic school than I, but this was a blessing in disguise because our teacher, Mr Bob Kean, was also a member of the Scottish Football Association at schoolboy level. He had seen me coming through and put me forward for trials at international level.

That time came when I was 14, but I had an awful trial. Those trials can make or break you, and although I played well in the first game I had such a shocker in the second that at half-time they took me off and put another lad on. 'That's it,' I thought. 'I've blown it.' So it came as a mighty relief when Mr Kean explained later: 'We already knew that some of the lads we took off at half-time would be in the squad and you were among those. We just wanted to have a look at some of the others about whom we were undecided.'

I was the proudest kid in Scotland. You had to buy your own blazer, but they gave you a pocket badge which proclaimed that you were a Scottish schoolboy international. I was always a bit bigger and stronger than others of my age, and I was first invited to Leeds United when I was just 13. The local scout for the Second Division team (about whom few people in Scotland had even heard) had seen me playing in the local league. In Scotland, Celtic and Rangers were the forerunners, while Hearts and Hibernian had useful teams. My local team, Dundee, were reasonable, but the big problem in Scottish football in those days was that the clubs had no facilities for kids and consequently few youngsters wanted to go to them.

Those who did joined the ground staff at the age of 15 and everybody knew what that meant: brushing the terraces and doing all the other mucky jobs around the ground. It was cheap labour. They did a bit of training, but once they had started there were only two choices. You either played in the reserves, which no ambitious 15-year-old wanted to do on a regular basis, or you played in the junior league, which was the equivalent of today's Vauxhall Conference. And again, playing at that level is a bit dangerous for a 15-year-old. You get the old pros who can be a bit nasty. It's not the ideal preparation or build-up for a kid to come through.

The attraction, then, of going to England, was that the clubs were properly set up with a definitive structure at every level. There were leagues in which you could play with and against your own age group and that way, on an equal footing, natural talent would shine through. This was what was so appealing to my father. In 1959 Leeds were a small club. They were mad keen to get this tall and skinny 13-year-old early and, with my parents, I travelled down on three or four occasions during school holidays. John Quinn, the chief scout, would come up to see me every weekend to keep me sweet and to give my mother a bottle of Harvey's Bristol Cream sherry and a dozen fresh eggs. The purpose of this was so that she could build up my frame and develop my strength. So I used to set off for school in a morning half-pissed because I'd had a rather large measure of sherry with a raw egg in it! This was how keen they were on me. The Leeds man would also give my father a fiver, which in those days was basically half his fisherman's wage, and I would get ten bob (50p). Few people had cars then and on Sunday mornings, when the bus pulled up, we knew that John should be on it. As the scheduled time approached, my father and I would anxiously look out of the window to see that he was getting off the bus; my father looking forward to his drinking money and me to the cash which would fund a trip into town for a good time with my mates.

My mother had two jobs (one of which was as housekeeper to the publishing magnate D.C. Thompson) because my father liked a drink. She got basic housekeeping from my father and he kept the rest for his drink and cigarettes, as was the practice in those days. In fairness to her, I had the best of everything. Anything I wanted was invariably produced and I have always held that debt to my mother. She was the one who came to every match. It was a bit embarrassing that the others all had their fathers there while it was my mum who was running up and down the line, shouting at the referee. She was fanatical then and has always remained so. The top and bottom of my father was that he drank too much. During the war he had been on German patrol in the North Sea, where all the boats were getting sunk, so he had come through a hard life, seeing a lot of his friends killed.

Afterwards his life was for the pub, not for the family. He was a generous man – too generous for his own good. When he came back off a fishing trip he would blow all his money buying drinks for his pals. But the war must have taken a great deal out of young men like him. Only a minority of people alive in Britain today know the horrors of war and, unfortunately, too many are too quick to forget about it. When Manchester United beat Bayern Munich 2–1 in the Champions League in 1999 there was a percentage of football fans who wanted a German team to defeat a British team, and that shows how quickly the dark days of war, and the unspeakable things which went on, have been obliterated from the mind.

There were traces of football history in my father's family but the strength of my lineage is on my mother's side. She was a member of the Duncan family, which was closely related to that of Mrs Elsie Revie, and the Duncans produced quite a few professional footballers. Few people were aware, and I did not let it be known, that I was distantly related to Mrs Revie. I did not want accusations flying that my joining Leeds was a question of keeping it in the family.

Much is made these days about team spirit being critical to the success of clubs and certainly, as far as Leeds United are concerned, that is true to an extent. But in my early days the camaraderie with all the lads was fabulous. You played for each other on the understanding that the only way you were going to better yourselves as ordinary people from common families was to be successful, and the only way you were going to be successful was to play as a team. I don't think that that is the mentality now. Modern players have all got massive contracts and they sulk a lot more easily.

My first big match was for Dundee schoolboys. I was 13 and playing for the Under-15s. We went to England, which was a massive thing to do then, and we played Derby County at their old Baseball Ground. You were talking a 14-hour trip on a bus down and I always remember going through Boroughbridge in Yorkshire, a bottleneck on the old A1, and there were traffic jams all over the place. We actually played under floodlights, which was an amazing experience. Later, I played against Perth schoolboys at St Johnstone, who also had lights at a time when all the clubs were getting them one by one. They were of a poor standard – a few lamps on a telegraph pole was the norm – but they were lights nonetheless and with the white ball it was just thrilling.

Only a few players, such as John Duncan, have come out of the Dundee area and made it to any decent level in the game. The former Aberdeen, Chelsea and Scotland player David Robb is another who springs to mind and it was a rare occurrence indeed that David and I, who played in the same Under-16 YMCA team, should end up in the same Scotland international team together. These representative games always attracted a posse of scouts. Leeds, who must have been forward-thinking to have had a scout as far away as Dundee, had already expressed their interest in me and I remember that Preston North End, a big club then, also had a 'spotter' in the area. In general, though, the big clubs waited until the internationals came along. The attitude was that they would just go along and take their pick.

I was called up to play for Scotland Schoolboys against England at Ibrox, and scored twice in a 4–2 win, and the next minute there were representatives from 30 clubs all parked in our street. Among them was Manchester United's Joe Armstrong, who left a briefcase in our home containing £5,000, a windfall which was gratefully recieved. In those days that was a small fortune. My parents could have bought a row of terraced houses with that kind of money. That kind of incentive, or inducement, was illegal and remains so, even though it still goes on in the game to a larger extent than many people realise.

When Leeds heard about this they could in no way afford to match the figure, and came up instead with £800 and a salary structure which put me on more money than most of the kids already at Elland Road. The senior pros had only just negotiated a deal which put them over the £20-a-week limit, but I joined for £17 a week, with the club paying my lodgings and giving me two juicy steaks a week to take home for my landlady to cook for me. I would send my mother £4 a week up to Scotland.

Typically, Rangers sent a messenger to say that I had been 'invited' to go to Ibrox for an interview with Mr Scott Symon, who was the manager at the time, and this supercilious attitude was precisely why people did not go there. It was 'We are Glasgow Rangers; you are honoured by our interest'. My mother, a strong Catholic, said frostily: 'Oh, we've been invited by Rangers have we? Just tell them you will never be going to Rangers.'

Similarly, Manchester United's attitude was: 'That's more money than you'll get from anybody else.' Had I not made it, the loss of their investment would not have been the biggest thing in the world to them. They were the club that everybody was following for sentimental reasons as much as anything in the wake of the recent Munich air disaster, attracting massive crowds wherever they went. I had, in fact, been down to Old Trafford, but nothing of any significance transpired until after that international, when they suddenly started to come on strong. I was leaving school within a month and plenty of clubs thought that they could just make a timely move and steamroller over little Leeds. There was not a club in Britain that didn't want to sign me.

I always listened to Mum and Dad. I wasn't the sort of person who would say 'I'm going here' or 'I'm doing that'. I left it mostly to them, in the knowledge that they would do the best for me, as they had always done. When I signed professional forms for Leeds they were given another £2,000. For an outlay of £2,800, Leeds got a player who made more than 700 appearances and scored over 200 goals. I became the youngest debutant in Leeds United's history when, at the age of 15 years and 289 days, I lined up against Southampton on 29 September 1962. In a 1–1 draw our forward line was: Lorimer, Storrie, Charles, Collins and Johanneson.

chapter two

BRIDGE OF SIGHS

WHEN I FIRST ARRIVED AT LEEDS AS A 15-YEAR-OLD I WAS PUT INTO LODGINGS run by Mrs Goodman at 69 Eastleigh Road with five other players: Norman Hunter, Terry Cooper, Clive Middlemass, Mick Addy and Robbie Nicholson. I didn't like that. Six blokes under one roof was just too stifling an environment for me, having come from a home in which there was just me and my brother. The teapot held six cups and it was always a race between us to gulp it down and try to squeeze an extra drop out of it. I couldn't be doing with that. They were all great lads – Norman and Terry went on to enjoy great careers while the other three were lesser lights in the game – but I was never happy there. At this time it was looking very much as though Norman would be released by the club. But Don Revie had taken over from Jack Taylor and had seen something in him which his predecessor had not.

I can remember watching Norman playing in the old-fashioned inside-forward position in a reserve game against Aston Villa at Elland Road, a match in which, funnily enough, George Graham played for Villa. We had only just met and I knew nothing about him, but as I brushed the terraces as part of my ground staff boy's duties with the match in progress, I looked at him a few times and thought, 'He's hopeless. He's never going to make it.' He was long-legged, weak, tall, slow; the very antithesis of an aspiring footballer. But what Don had seen was a boy with a great attitude, a good left foot and a win-at-all-costs mentality. He made him into a wonderful back-four player, one of the best the game has ever seen. This was the vision of the man. Not only was Norman an inside-forward, but Paul Reaney and Terry Cooper were wingers. Under Don, they finished up along with Big Jack Charlton as our back-four. He transformed all of them from ordinary forwards into brilliant defenders.

At the time that Revie was busily formulating his team plans, I was desperate to get out of Eastleigh Road. Billy Bremner, who knew that I was unhappy, announced that he was getting married in the summer. He was in great digs with Mrs Silcott in Sandhurst Terrace and if I bided my time I could replace him there. Mrs Silcott had a son who was a bus driver and very rarely there, so she basically adopted me. The only trouble was that I was in the attic room, which was three floors up. In the winter, with no heating, I would wake up each day to see my exhaled breath and the window frozen over. But my landlady was kind and caring and would make sure I went upstairs to bed with a flask of coffee and a hot water bottle. Despite her best efforts, I had been spoiled by my mother when living at home and was unused to these conditions. I soon came to realise, though, that if you were going to be a footballer you would have to put up with these inconveniences. I would go home every six weeks and each time the train pulled out of the station to cross the Tay Bridge it was only a matter of seconds before I was in floods of tears. I would look back down the river until the Broughty Castle promontory had disappeared from view and I could not choke back the emotion of once again leaving behind my home comforts for my stand-alone existence in Yorkshire. I had to straighten myself out because of the embarrassment of crying in front of the rest of the passengers, and usually by the first stop down the track, at Leuchars, I was composed again.

In retrospect it is easy to understand why homesickness overcame so many kids in those days. It was rife. The working conditions at English clubs left a lot to be desired. After a Saturday match you were handed a brush and told to continue with your chores until the stadium was spotless. That included mucking out toilets, and it was usually while this task was being performed that you would say to yourself: 'What's all this about? I'm supposed to be a footballer.' What it amounted to was cheap labour. Brushing the terraces, usually in the freezing cold and pissing rain, was your first job of the day. Then you'd be given some respite to do half an hour's training before it was back onto the steps until three o'clock in the afternoon. No luxuries there, then. But, looking back, I think that regime was what gave you the mental strength to become a footballer. These days, as far as I know, the academy kids don't have any menial chores to do and have the comfort of a massive wage, excellent accommodation, food cooked by chefs and first-class recreational facilities.

I had arrived at Elland Road in a blaze of publicity about this kid from Scotland whom Leeds had beaten all these other clubs in the race to sign up, and there was some resentment among my fellow lodgers because they knew that I was being paid more than they were. The other factor was that they were paying rent and I was not, so purely on budgetary considerations I was able to spend and do a lot more than they could manage. But the older players would know nothing of my proximity to them on the wage scale. Big Jack Charlton was the senior pro as far as I was concerned, but also at Elland Road were Tommy Younger and Bobby Collins. Bobby was the man whom Don had brought in from Everton as his on-the-pitch general. He was a hard taskmaster who would kick you up the arse and give you a cuff round the ear if he thought that you were not pulling your weight in training. I once saw him do that to Albert Johanneson in a match, never mind to the kids in training. He was a wonderful tutor. The things I learned from Bobby in terms of what you had to be like to be a pro, the sacrifices you have to make, were unquantifiable.

Jack, on the other hand, was a law unto himself. He was anti-circuits, anti-cross-country runs, anti-training of any kind, really. When I first went down they'd put a circuit out and the senior pros would simply throw the mats and the benches and the like down the embankment at the training headquarters at Fullerton Park. 'We're not having any of this,' they would say. It was something Don had to sort out. The attitude had to change under him. Cross-country for Jack meant being in last position, getting a lift in a passing truck and smoking a fag, having been dropped off at the corner and waiting until the rest of us emerged. Billy Bremner was much the same. He'd say about cross-country, because he wasn't any good at it: 'We shouldn't be doing this. This isn't part of training.'

Tommy Younger, our excellent keeper who had also played for Liverpool and Scotland as well as the great Hibernian team I had watched as a kid, Cliff Mason, Grenville Hair and Eric Smith were other seasoned pros at the club and their idea of professionalism was totally different to the one which prevails these days. To them it was just a joke: they could play football and they could get a wage out of it, so that was that. There was no proper preparation for matches or dedication to duty. On the night that the Tottenham player John White was killed by lightning while playing golf, Big Jack had asked me to babysit for him. I did so with some girl. Neither of us had a car and Jack said that he would drive me home. He was notorious for borrowing a fiver here and a tenner there and never paying it back and on the way, emboldened by my belief that he would feel indebted to me for my babysitting duties, I asked for the return of the fiver I had loaned him a couple of weeks previously. I should have known better. 'Fiver?' he queried. 'You've had the use of my couch all night with your girlfriend.'

I suppose it was cheaper than the Hilton, but we could have had bed and breakfast for a fiver!

That was Jack through and through. When we were given our tickets for international matches – these were docked from our wages – Jack would go to everybody and say he would buy them and throw in a few bob extra because he had so many people to cater for. It was nearly an impossible task after the match in question to get him to cough up for their face value, never mind the promised bonus. It was certainly no good going up to him individually, because he would just shoo you away, so we had to form a posse. Even then, he would fling some money on the table, saying: 'I'm sick of this. Sort it out between you.' Some of the lads were only earning £10, and if £4 had gone for two tickets they were pretty desperate to get it back. Jack was a great character. Both he and Billy liked to go to The Woodman, their local pub at Halton, and take up residence in the domino room where they would enjoy a few pints with the lads. They both smoked and so it was little wonder that neither enjoyed cross-country running. Also, they were in among some terrific athletes. Albert Johanneson would set off like a puma homing in on its prey, with everybody shouting, as he started to disappear from view: 'Slow down, Albert. Give us a chance!'

Eddie Gray, who was a good runner, got himself really fit one summer and was hell-bent on beating Albert. With the winning post in sight, Eddie, who was in front, had put in so much effort that he collapsed in a heap and was passed by everybody, even the stragglers, as our trainer Les Cocker tried to bring him round. Eddie was the joke of that week, but here were two contrasting attitudes. Seventeen-year-old Eddie wanted to put everything into it and do his best, while old-timer Jack's attitude was: 'Look at Albert. Daft bastard. Let him run. We're not bothered. We'll lob along at the back and get there in our own time.'

Don's attitude was that pre-season training was like putting money in the bank. It was building stamina and strength and toning up muscles and the work you put into pre-season would carry you through the next ten months. It was not in the make-up of the old pros to accept this. The reason I got into the first team at 15 was that Billy had gone up to Scotland and married Vicky who, just like I had been, was very homesick when they came to Leeds. She wanted to live in Scotland and Billy, who was only 20, wanted away, aiming to join a Scottish club. It looked like he was going to sign for Hibernian, but Leeds put a massive fee (in the region of £45,000) on his head and that, for one so young, was a fortune. Every time he went up to Scotland he was late back because of the problem with Vicky. Leeds so nearly lost Billy, and who knows where the Revie plan would have gone without him? Had Hibernian come up with the money Billy would definitely have left, but their loss was very definitely Leeds United's gain.

People think you go to a football club as a kid and it is all roses, but that is simply not the case. Lads of your own age outside of the game go out and spend from Friday to Sunday having a great time in social surroundings, but in my day you couldn't go out after Wednesday when a Saturday game was upcoming. At the age of 17, both Eddie Gray and myself were in the first team, and there was no way you could break the club curfews. The club rules said that you were not allowed to be seen in a bar or any other licensed premises for 48 hours before a game, so that if we played on Wednesday you could have a drink after the game but not on Thursday and Friday. Then you could go out on Saturday night and maybe Sunday, but not Monday or Tuesday, because of the next Wednesday match.

Revie was unequivocal about this to the extent that he would have spies about the city and would ring your landlady to check your whereabouts. He was so thorough and knew everything that was going on. He had the city of Leeds covered and there was no getting away with anything. It filtered through the ranks. If Brian, the trainer, told you to get out there and cut the grass that is what you had to do. And if you gave the groundsman some stick, or complained, or told him to fuck off, you were straight in front of the manager. The result was a fine. It seems harsh, and probably was, but you only have to look at what happened to Leeds United under Don Revie's leadership to be forced to concede that it was the right way. But you try telling a 15-year-old kid that that is the right way. My mother does not know to this day that I used to cry going over that bridge. If she had known, there would have been no second crossings.

Even at that tender age I could not understand why I was not playing in the first team. I looked at them, and, no disrespect to players like Jimmy Storrie and others, I thought I was better than them. And I was. As far as Don was concerned, though, I was just a youngster. What killed me was that when we got to the FA Cup final against Liverpool in 1965 I had been at Elland Road for three years and was just beginning to get into the team on a regular basis. As soon as I signed pro forms I cracked a bone in my leg and was six months, a longer time than normal, in getting over it. But I had played the last few games of the season and felt sure that I was going to get into the team for Wembley. There were no substitutes then and I believed that I would be chosen ahead of Storrie. But Don basically elected to stick with the team which had got them there and there was just no consoling me when the team was announced. In the game itself Jim and Albert Johanneson never played. They froze and it became a complete embarrassment. I was just watching and shaking my head throughout. A tortuous game which required extra time to settle, with Liverpool eventually winning 2–1.

When Eddie Gray came down a year after me he had the same attitude. He was all quality and felt he should be in the team straightaway, but Don always preached the virtue of patience. 'Your turn will come, son,' he would say, not wanting to rush things. And sure enough the chance came, though never quickly enough. They call players young these days at 19, 20 and 21 – my career was half finished by then! At 21 I thought I was getting on a bit. An old pro. I'd been playing for six years and the general way of things then was that at 17 if you were good enough, you were old enough. You were in. Nowadays they go very gingerly with young players, starting them off at 19 or 20. By 27 or 28 they are at the veteran stage and by the age of 30 everybody is saying: 'It's time they got rid of him.' Careers are shorter. I can't think of many great players from my day – Giles, Bremner, Dalglish, Gray – who were not playing first-team football at 17. Howard Kendall played in a cup final at 16; Trevor Francis when he was just a kid. Joe Cole would be one modern-day example, but he is certainly the exception rather than the rule.

If joining a club involved intricate finances then leaving could be even more fraught. It was standard practice at Leeds that they asked for £40,000 from whichever club a player was joining. They did not have the decency to address the issue of what an individual had done for the club over a period of years. To my mind, most or all of this £40,000 should really have gone to the player in question. In my own case, 16 years down the track from when I first walked into Elland Road, I dug my heels in and swore to the manager (Jimmy Adamson) that I would never leave as long as they were seeking money for me. The principle was wrong, but it was nevertheless applied to the likes of John Giles and Norman Hunter as well. It was very sad that the club had that attitude. When challenged about it, Manny Cussins, the chairman, would say: 'You've been paid down the years, haven't you?' I would even have accepted the £2,800 I cost them in the first place and called it a draw. There was just no appreciation by the men at the top for your efforts on their behalf. Of course, Don Revie had left by then and the new men at the top had no feelings for you. In fact, they wanted you out.

I went to Toronto, having stood firm at Leeds for two months over the money issue. As far as I know they got nothing, and indeed I would hate to think that they had got anything. When, at the age of 17, you signed your professional forms the club owned you lock, stock and barrel. They could put you out of the game, which they threatened to do to lots of players, and the whole attitude towards the players was bad.

I cannot say one bad thing about Don after the way in which he looked after us and fought for us to get the best he could. But he was unusual in that respect and that is why I now say good luck to the players with their big salaries and high-flying lifestyles. They are getting their own back. Maybe if directors in the old days had been a bit fairer there would have been no need for players' unions to fight for what they have got. They have much to thank George Eastham for in his fight with Newcastle which led to him going on strike in pursuit of the £20-a-week minimum.

Directors were ogres. When John Charles scored a hat-trick for Leeds at Hull in only his second game at centre-forward, having started at centre-half, old Sam Bolton, who was the chairman, was waiting back at Elland Road with the manager, Major Buckley. 'Fabulous,' Sam said. 'Go down to my garage and get three gallons of petrol – one for each goal.'

'What good's three gallons of petrol to me, Mr Chairman?' said John. 'I haven't got a car.' This was the attitude of the board. They thought they were making a wonderful gesture.

It was much the same at international level for Scotland. You would get a letter congratulating you on being picked to play for your country and this was accompanied by all the rules. You couldn't speak to the press. You were allowed second-class rail travel, in my case from Leeds to Glasgow. You were expected in Glasgow no later than half past ten on the Saturday night, which meant that you had to go straight from your game that afternoon. You were allowed one buffet meal, which amounted to a sandwich and a cup of tea. No visits to the dining car for us. A taxi was permitted, and this was underlined, only if necessary. If you could get a bus from Elland Road to the train then for the good of your country, saving them a bit of money, you were expected to do so.

In clashes between Scotland and England there would be 132,000 spectators at Hampden and 100,000 at Wembley, yet we were each allowed two match tickets. You bought the rest. I would ring my mum and say: 'I'm in the team against England.' This, of course, was the greatest honour for any family and she would say: 'Great, son. We're all coming.'

'How many is "all" mum?'

'Forty.'

Tickets cost £2.50 then. Your match fee was £100 less tax, so you came out with £50. All those people watching, all that revenue and the match beamed live on television around the world, yet you got £50. You couldn't expect your aunties and uncles, grandads and grandmas, to pay. You were the big important footballer. So you shelled out £100 on match tickets for them. It doesn't take a mathematical genius to work out that, in the final analysis, it had cost you £50 to play for your country.

This was when the card games first came into football. You had to win at cards to clear your expenses! I had to laugh when the controversy surrounding Kevin Keegan, his England team and card schools was whipped up. A big issue was made of £5,000 being staked on the turn of a card. These players are earning £35,000 a week so all that was at stake was one-seventh of their wages. We were three weeks *behind* through the purchase of tickets and it really was desperation stakes. And if you lost at cards as well there were major, serious problems. No actual money was involved in the games – you didn't carry it – and the profits and losses were noted on a piece of paper. So for some weeks afterwards you would be sending money to the player to whom you were in debt. Of course, we were paid weekly in cash, so you'd send £50 one week and another £50 the next. If you won a match you'd be able to syphon it out of your bonus and send it off without the wife knowing.

The Scotland team hotel was the Queens at Largs. This was an old-fashioned guest-house, with ten bedrooms and a bath on each floor to accommodate 20 players. We would return from training sessions soaking wet and filthy with mud to impossible conditions, taking our turn in cooling, filthy water, while the SFA members were in the best hotel in Glasgow enjoying their gin and tonics with ice and a twist of lemon. Little wonder that the worm turned. How long did they think that players, honoured as they were to play for their country, would endure such an imbalance?

chapter three

DIRTY LEEDS

THE ATTITUDE OF THE OLDER PLAYERS LIKE BOBBY COLLINS, JACK CHARLTON and Billy Bremner in European competition was something to behold. My first game in Europe was in the Inter Cities Fairs Cup in Turin, a match in which Collins was to break his thigh. I was just 17 and playing on the wing and while my feeling was not one of fear I was certainly cautious. In those days the Italians were filthy and nasty with it. The tackling was awful; it really was. It was a question for them of quickly sorting out the men from the boys and the number of vicious, ferocious tackles that Bobby went into was criminal. It was the hardest of schools to be brought up in. Yet it was all great experience for us. Norman Hunter didn't need any tutoring in how to kick somebody, but all the same there were lessons to be learned about the cynical side of the game.

The learning process was not confined to the fields of Europe, either, for the emerging Leeds team. In my first game against Liverpool at Anfield I was up against that colossus of a man, Ron Yeats. I had the audacity to score in the first five minutes in front of the Kop. On a frozen pitch Gilesy hit a shot and Tommy Lawrence, their goalkeeper, dived to stop it and I hit the rebound into the roof of the net. Our game plan was that when they hit a free kick from deep all the big guys would go back to defend and I would be left alone up front so that they would be forced to keep two back. One of these was Big Ron, and as our boys pumped the ball forward I went past him only to be felled by a staggering right hook. It hit me right in the solar plexus and as I went down I feared I was dying. I could not breathe. Our trainer, Les Cocker, came flying on, never said a word to Ron but said to me: 'Maybe now you'll fucking learn to keep away from the big boys.' This was the school we were in. There was no sympathy. As far as Les was concerned this was a salutary lesson. One minute I was thinking I was the dog's bollocks, having scored a precious goal, and the next I was getting a bollocking.

My first game at Bolton was much the same. They had two notoriously aggressive full-backs in Roy Hartle and Ralph Banks. The left-back, Banks, was at the end of his career and my attitude was: 'You old twat. I'll give you a right chasing here.' Early in the game I knocked the ball past him on the outside, flew past him and crossed for us to score.

'You do that again,' said Banks, 'and I'll have you.' It was no idle threat. Soon afterwards I tried a similar trick and, sure enough, the next thing I remember was picking myself up off the cinder track. He'd hit me so hard that I went up in the air and landed flat on my back. I was seeing stars, but again all I got was a bollocking. 'Next time somebody tells you that,' said Cocker, 'maybe you'll listen to him.' I didn't go down the line again. I cut inside.

Different experiences all help in the moulding of a young footballer and I certainly had a very unusual adventure when I was picked for the Scotland amateur team to tour Kenya. It's a quiz question in Scotland these days that there is only one player ever to represent the country at every level – schoolboy, youth, amateur, Under-23 and full – and that is yours truly. The trip to Kenya was undertaken in 1963 in order to celebrate their independence. I was still only 16 – I actually celebrated my 17th birthday on the tour – and it was a great honour for me to travel with the older guys in the team who were mainly playing for Queen's Park in the Scottish Second Division. They were always an amateur team, made up of professional people like doctors and lawyers, and still are. One member of this team was Andy Roxburgh, who would go on to become Scotland manager some years later. Although it was exciting, being so far from home in unfamiliar surroundings did bring elements of fear. In the middle of one night in Nairobi I was startled awake by the presence of somebody in the room. It was a little black boy and I thought 'Oh my God'. But this was in the days when they had servants, and he had only come along to take away my shoes to be cleaned.

The first match on tour was against Kenya and this attracted a massive crowd, with all the tribes descending from all points north, south, east and west to celebrate this momentous declaration of independence. The sheer size of the crowd was frightening in itself, but during the match I was aware of some commotion in their midst. I asked one of their English-speaking players what was going on and he said: 'Don't worry. The witch doctor has arrived. He's the guru around here.'

Fortunately this individual didn't cast any spells on us. We won the tournament, and I scored a few goals. I learned a lot from these older men and it was something that made me grow up. They got me rat-arsed on the local brew and tried to line me up with one of the local ladies of the night. I resisted that. We had been warned not to wander too far from our accommodation and, anyway, I wouldn't have been capable in my prevailing state. It was an exciting time because I knew that on my return from the tour I would be signing my professional forms. This was done without delay. Since that Southampton début I was taken along steadily, playing in a couple of League Cup games, and I now felt fully prepared to launch myself into the game. But within a month of signing I cracked my shin-bone in the semi-final of a junior cup game on the main pitch at Elland Road. The keeper dived over my leg and I spent six weeks of the summer in plaster.

The injury meant a slow start to my first season. My recovery took longer than was typical for that kind of setback and some of the blame for that must go to our trainer Les Cocker. Freddie Goodwin, who was playing for us then, had suffered a really bad leg break and wore a calliper to aid his rehabilitation. Les got us both together in training and produced a medicine ball, urging us to put our weight into a tackle. We both shivered as we made contact with the ball and as we came out of the tackle I hit Freddie's calliper with my leg. We were both rolling about in agony and that had a significant effect on my game. My confidence going into the tackle was shattered and it wasn't until three months before the end of the season that I got into the side. Even then I didn't think Don should put me in because I wasn't playing well enough. His philosophy, however, seemed to be that he would pick me for a match where there was a big crowd, showing his confidence in me. The chosen fixture was a Yorkshire derby against Sheffield Wednesday at Elland Road. They had a big, rough centre-half called Vic Mobley, a real tough guy, and, true to form, in the first minute of the game there was a 50–50 involving him and me. I thought 'Here we go', but I came out of the tackle fine, although he won the ball.

It ended as a wasted 1964–65 season for me; in and out of the team, confidence gone and no place in the Cup final line-up. Many was the time I thought about going home. I wasn't playing regularly, I couldn't see my leg getting better and I seemed to be losing the battle with my willpower. All the same I got through it and I stayed. Still only 17, I was in the side from the first kick of the new season and my career was under way in earnest. I finished the campaign as leading scorer with 19 goals. Having finished runners-up in the league the previous season we were in the Inter Cities Fairs Cup, so I was to get an early taste of European action, firstly in Turin. Ten minutes into the game Bobby Collins suffered a thoroughly dreadful injury and that was a bitter blow to everybody. He had been the greatest influence on the side, having been brought in by Don for £25,000 from Everton to marshal this crop of youngsters. He needed an experienced player with drive and Bobby was the man.

We won the two-leg tie 2–1 on aggregate, holding Turin to a

goalless draw over there, and that was no mean performance. To go to Italy and match one of their teams in their own back yard was regarded as something special, and it was that game which saw the transformation of the team. Johnny Giles had been outside and I was playing inside-forward, but the injury to Bobby meant that a new general was needed. So Johnny moved inside from the wing, which he always hated, and I eventually went out wide. The winger Mick O'Grady was brought in from Huddersfield but unfortunately he was always prone to injury. Bobby made a remarkable recovery for a man of 36, but his involvement in the game from that point was only spasmodic.

After disposing of Turin we were drawn against Leipzig and, unlike today, when British teams playing in Europe can be back home in their beds before midnight, this involved a real trek. Then, to play an East German team, you flew to the West and got on a bus to the border at Checkpoint Charlie. Once on the other side you got onto an East German bus which would be rust on wheels and be driven along pot-holed roads for two and a half hours in the snow as your first glimpse of the communist bloc. A conversation between more than two of the local people was viewed as a conspiracy, so you saw very few people about. It was all very austere and quite unnerving. It was on this trip that Don's professionalism came to the fore. He insisted upon taking our own food, like baked beans and steak and chicken, and a chef, leaving nothing to chance.

There had been six inches of snow overnight, but there was never any question of matches being called off in those conditions. All they did was to pack the snow and put blue lines on it, with an orange ball in use. We played in studs and Don and his coaching staff had shaved off the bottom layer of the leather so that the nails poked through, allowing us to get a foothold on the ice. They knew our studs would be checked, so on each of them they affixed a cardboard tip to hide the nails. We kicked off the cardboard as we came out for the kick-off. Within minutes blood was oozing from all of their players' legs and they were complaining furiously to the referee. Their protests fell on deaf ears, with the official insisting that he had already checked our boots. We won the game 2–1, with goals from myself and Billy Bremner, in front of a sparse crowd of just 8,000.

Gamesmanship, bribery and corruption were rife in the European game in those days and Don knew that if you were to survive you would have to match them misdeed for misdeed. There were gold watches for referees before games and at Elland Road I have seen a bottle of whisky for the ref plus a present for himself and his wife. When you played abroad as an English team you got nothing. You had to fight for everything and you had to win well to get a result. You'd go away not to lose or to nick a goal and bring them back to finish off the job in the second leg. These experiences were invaluable enough, but there was also much to learn on the domestic front. Running out at White Hart Lane to face the great Bill Nicholson Tottenham side for the first time was exhilarating for me. Three of the players in opposition, Dave Mackay, Bill Brown and Alan Gilzean, were heroes to me as a kid growing up in Scotland. Despite this I wasn't in awe of them, although they were the great team of the age, and I even got one of our goals in a 3–2 defeat. This, more than anything, was confirmation of my arrival on the scene; to be on the same park as those mighty players.

Back in Europe our next date produced the most remarkable game against Valencia at Elland Road, refereed by the revered Dutchman Leo Horne. He took all 22 players off the pitch after an incident involving Jack Charlton sparked a mass brawl. Whenever we got a corner it was Jack's habit to stand right by the goalkeeper. I would bend them in from the left and Eddie Gray from the right and, being so tall, Jack always had a chance. On this occasion he ended up in a shoving match with the keeper, who committed the cardinal sin of spitting in Jack's face. Now when Jack's head went, it went completely. He went ballistic, and you could see the fear in the keeper's eyes. He turned and ran, with Jack in hot pursuit, towards the corner flag, where he found himself with two choices. He either jumped into the crowd, among a sea of baying Leeds fans, or he turned to face an incandescent Jack. He chose the latter, getting a hefty smack for his troubles, but if I had been in his boots I think I would have taken my chance with the Leeds fans!

The match was held up for 11 minutes and it was then that the club acquired its 'Dirty Leeds' tag. In fact, what was great about this particular side was that it could play all teams any way they wanted to. If a team wanted to play them at football Leeds could outplay them. If they thought for one minute that they could play the dirty stuff and Leeds would bottle it then they were very quickly put right. This reputation spread very quickly throughout Europe and we were given the respect we deserved to the extent that some of the results we achieved on our travels were quite phenomenal.

Having drawn 1–1 at home to Valencia we beat them away, 1–0, and then we were drawn in the semi-final against Ujpest Dosza. The Hungarians had some terrific players, notably their bald-headed winger Beni. Don had had them watched two or three times and reported that they really were something special; the best. We beat them 4–1 at Elland Road with an exquisite performance and we wondered what the boss had been talking about. But when we got over there they absolutely pulverised us for half an hour. Gary Sprake, our young goalkeeper, was flinging himself left and right to make last-second saves, they were hitting the post, hitting the bar and missing by inches. But they didn't score. I was up front alone against two defenders, dummied to let the ball run between my legs on the halfway line, wrong-footing them, and ran 50 yards to tuck the ball home. Their heart went then. That was the end of the argument. But what a belting we took from that team. This was what you found in Europe. The teams were Jekyll and Hyde, going at you hell for leather until they went a goal down, when their heads went down.

After most of these European games it was customary to attend a banquet, at which gifts were exchanged between the clubs. Nowadays the players are straight onto the plane heading back home, but because of the vast distances and the length of time taken to get to these venues more was made of the fixture. In Ujpest the atmosphere out there on the pitch had been quite heated and now, in the function room, some stern glances were being cast upon our table by the Hungarians. A feeling of deep unease was developing as we returned the icy stares and after the banquet one or two of our lads got outside to find a menacing group of waiting Ujpest players who clearly wanted to take the game a bit further. A brawl developed and, never ones to back away from a challenge, our players got stuck in to the extent that when the rest of our party emerged the sight which confronted them was one of several Hungarians running hell for leather along the left bank of the Danube. It was the perfect finish to a perfect day!

We all went back for a few drinks in the team hotel. There were no nightclubs to speak of in the eastern bloc, so our hotels were the focal point of our entertainment. It was funny watching the attempts by the old directors to procure a local lady of the night as they became more and more inebriated, and the fervent hopes of the young single players were that when it became apparent to the directors that they would be incapable of any activity with these ladies they would pass them on to them to finish off the job they had started.

In the final, against Real Zaragoza, it finished all square after the two legs and went to a third game. We won 1–0 over there and they beat us 2–1 at Elland Road. The away goals rule was not yet in force and on the toss of a coin the decider was to be at Elland Road. They were a good side, with a liberal smattering of excellent Brazilian players, but we really fancied our chances of lifting the trophy in front of our own supporters. On a really warm spring day we watched them train at Fullerton Park. The pitch was very hard and they looked awesome in the sunshine with their overhead kicks, body-swerving and boxes of tricks. Don was thinking: 'I'm not having any of this.' In the afternoon we went to bed in the team hotel dreaming of impending glory, and when we arrived at the ground Don's first instruction was to go out and look at the pitch and make sure we had the right studs in our boots.

We were perplexed. Studs? We always played in moulded ones on the hard surfaces, but Don had had other ideas. While we were in dreamland he had summoned the Fire Brigade down to flood the pitch with thousands of gallons of water. It was like a quagmire. The Spaniards were not amused. They complained bitterly to anyone who would listen, but Don merely shrugged his shoulders and told them: 'It's been terrible. This afternoon there was a torrential thunderstorm and this area was hit by flash floods.' Everywhere but the pitch was bone dry and there were furious arguments, but his attempts to slow down the Brazilian contingent backfired horribly. We lost the game 3–1. When we had got over the disappointment the joke among the lads, never within Don's earshot of course, was: 'Just as well he watered the pitch, otherwise it would have been ten!'

It had been some first season for me. We were runners-up to Liverpool in the league, and runners-up in the Inter Cities Fairs Cup. This was only Leeds' second season back in the top flight, and having finished runners-up to Manchester United in the league and getting to the FA Cup final, the overall message to the rest of the teams out there was that Leeds under Don Revie were here to stay as a major force in English football.

chapter four

REVIE'S WORD IS LAW

JUST ROUND THE CORNER FROM MY DIGS IN LEEDS LIVED A LOCAL GIRL, Gillian Price, whom I started courting at the age of 17. This didn't settle me down completely, although it provided another interest in my new environment. Gillian was a trainee beautician. Her family always made me feel most welcome and I was able to pop round for a cup of tea in a normal family environment. Her father Les was an ex-paratrooper and was always interesting to talk to. He had an interest in sport and had been a PTI in the services. He helped me with my overall fitness, impressing upon me the benefits of using light weights, and I was always grateful for his contribution to my physical development. I was grateful, too, for his house rules, which decreed that Gillian must be home by half past nine every night after our visit to one of the coffee bars or the pictures. This was just about the time that the rest of the lads were beginning their social activities, so I would walk her up the hill, say goodnight and be off round the corner like a rocket to get the bus into town.

Like every lad of my age I wanted a car and for some time I had been looking admiringly at the bubble-type Hillman Minx owned by our then full-back Willie Bell. A thrifty Scotsman, Willie had looked after this old car. It was immaculate, and his pride and joy. He sold it to me for £130 and gave me a month to pay. My joy at this acquisition was unconfined, and though the original intention was for me to have a course of lessons I decided after an hour of instruction that I was sufficiently qualified to drive and I did so for 18 months without a licence. Eddie Gray and Jimmy Lumsden had come down from Scotland to join the club and they were great pals. We soon got together as friends. We liked the same things, football above all else, and we would jump into this little car and go off to a football match of our choosing wherever it might be and at whatever level. It might be Oldham, just over the Pennines, or a little reserve fixture somewhere in Yorkshire, and we would just bowl up to the ground. We'd get fish and chips, with a can of something to drink, on the way back and in a very short space of time what had been a wonderful specimen of a car became a tip. It also acquired dent after dent on our travels and Willie would see it in the car park the next day and dissolve into tears.

But we were happy. We lived for football and were brave enough one day to set off to watch a match in Scotland. We set off for Hampden straight after training and we had not journeyed far when a red light came on on the dashboard. I knew nothing about cars, except that they got you from A to B, but I did wonder why this hitherto unseen illumination should suddenly reveal itself. We reached our destination all right and watched the match untroubled by such trivia as this red light, but on the return journey my headlights were becoming dimmer by the mile. By the time we reached Carlisle driving had become totally impossible, so we pulled over. A lorry driver kindly stopped to help and after his inspection he revealed that the dynamo had gone. He was able to fix it, he said, but just as he was in the act a police car drew behind. We were very edgy, but it's funny what not having a driving licence in these circumstances will do for the politeness of your demeanour. It required a push for the car to start, the battery having gone completely flat, and everybody present, the two policemen included, heaved the car up an incline so that the engine would hopefully turn over as I let it freewheel back down again. The first attempt failed, so the party, already breathless, got me back up the hill. When I let it go there was nothing, and a final futile attempt was embarked upon; leaving footballers, policemen and a good Samaritan on their knees, gasping for breath. It was no good, one of them said. The car was knackered and we would have to contact a garage. It was only while we were waiting for them that it occurred to me that perhaps the ignition had to be switched on for a jump start to be effective. 'Quick, lads!' I shouted. 'Get in. I hadn't switched on!' It worked first time, and we zoomed out of Cumbria at 100 mph, fervently hoping that we would not be followed by a lot of irate people, some of them in uniform.

Another time I had a spot of car trouble came after one of the regular games of Scalextric we played at Eddie Gray's digs. The aim of this game was to get round a lap of a motor racing circuit faster than your opponent by means of a hand-held electronic drive. It provided many a happy night's entertainment with no little amount of money won and lost through betting on our individual skills. The game over, I said my goodbyes and got into my Hillman Minx which was parked outside. As I reversed, I could not understand why my pals were waving so frantically. How many goodbyes did they want? The reason for their non-stop waving soon became apparent when I reversed at 40 mph right into the front of a gleaming new Austin 1100 which the owner had taken round straight from the garage to show to his sister. The whole of the front end was caved in and within seconds this man was in floods of tears. I was in a dodgy position. I had no licence and my insurance had been arranged through my brother on the basis that, being a learner, I would always be accompanied. We managed to get the claim through, but though this was just another little bump on my car, for the other guy it was a disaster.

Although we were a bit on the wild side growing up it was in a good way. There was never any evil intent. We were just normal lads, more into high jinks than high drama. It was the start of a friendship with Eddie and Jimmy which remains to this day. Eddie joined me in the first team on the other wing as a 17-year-old and the competition for places was intense. Mick O'Grady had come in from Huddersfield and Jimmy Greenhoff from Barnsley, though Jimmy was soon involved in a shocking motoring accident on the York road. A lorry pulled across him and he finished up right underneath this big vehicle with the roof of his car taken clean off. He was in hospital with bad head injuries for a considerable time. This served as a warning considering my own motoring habits and I became a more responsible driver because of it. Jimmy, meanwhile, could not break into the team on a regular basis and left us after only a couple of years for Birmingham. By now Terry Cooper, Paul Madeley and Paul Reaney had all established themselves, with Johnny Giles having moved into midfield, and Don's jigsaw was coming into place. The team that would stay together for the next 15 years was taking shape. Nobody knew what glories lay ahead, but what was obvious was that this team contained a lot of special talent.

The transformation that Revie brought about in such a short time, particularly the repositioning of three forwards who looked as though they wouldn't make it, was remarkable. They were now pushing for Under-23 caps as defenders and this made everybody realise that we were playing under a special kind of manager. Discipline was hardly a byword in football clubs, yet it existed at Leeds United in no uncertain terms. It was a strict rulebook regime. There were times when you wondered if it was possible to pass wind on the way to the newsagents in a morning without one of Don's informers relating the fact.

The 1966–67 season saw us finish fourth in the league, beaten in the semi-final of the FA Cup, beaten in the final of the Inter Cities Fairs Cup by Dynamo Zagreb and dumped out of the League Cup in the fourth round by West Ham by the embarrassing scoreline of 7–0. I was fortunate enough not to have played that night through injury, as was our goalkeeper Gary Sprake, whose absence gave David Harvey one of his first senior appearances. I was at Upton Park, however, and it was one of those games in which absolutely everything clicked for the home side.

None of it was David's fault. It was just that West Ham, with Budgie Byrne, Geoff Hurst, Martin Peters, John Sissons and Bobby Moore, were simply awesome. They tore us apart, and it was one of those nights when everybody heard the result and said: 'You're joking. Leeds must have played all their reserves.' The fact was that we had not played second-stringers. Big Jack got a real chasing from Byrne and things were so bad that Mick Bates, just a kid, was sent on from the bench with the instruction from Don: 'Right, son, get your tracksuit off, go on and enjoy it.' Quite how you derive pleasure from something like that is beyond me and Mick's response of 'Oh, thanks boss' just about summed it up. But the controversy surrounding that match was as nothing compared with the semi-final of the FA Cup against Chelsea. At Villa Park we were 1–0 down with three minutes to go and the Welsh referee Ken Burns awarded us a free kick for a foul on me. Chelsea lined up their wall and from 30 yards I hit it straight over them into the top corner, leaving their goalkeeper Peter Bonetti sprawling and sparking great joy in our camp and among the Leeds fans. Chelsea heads were down, we were celebrating, and all of a sudden Burns instructed: 'Take it again. I didn't blow my whistle.' I am still asked to this day why the goal was disallowed and the fact is that I do not know. You see examples nowadays of quick free kicks being taken, goals being scored and no questions asked, so you can imagine our incredulity.

There was other sadness that year. Of course, England won the World Cup and, for a Scotsman, that was a bitter pill to have to swallow. Our Scottish contingent would go everywhere hoping that the train would come off the tracks, but with every passing match it was looking more and more like they would win it. It was a summer tinged with sadness. We knew that when the Leeds players came back from World Cup duty we would get it rammed down our throats forever, but the fortunate thing from our perspective was that we beat England 3–2 at Wembley in a European Championship qualifier soon afterwards and delighted in calling ourselves the unofficial world

PETER LORIMER

champions. Don rather liked all the banter and competitiveness that the World Cup evoked and decided that it might be a good idea in training to have our own mini-tournament involving players from different nationalities up against each other. We had enough in the squad to facilitate this, but what he didn't realise was the extent of the needle that England's success had brought about. Within a minute of the start of the Leeds United version of England versus Scotland a fight had broken out and there were two players heading for the treatment room, so this bright idea was quickly abandoned and it was back to the cross-country running to get rid of our pent-up energies.

The fifth round of the FA Cup was to bring about a titanic struggle with Sunderland. We drew 1–1 at Roker Park and it was the same result in the replay at Elland Road in a fixture which was to attract the all-time record gate of 57,892. So many people were crammed in that a wall in the main stand gave way. On this winter's evening straw had been laid on the pitch and its surroundings – there was no undersoil heating in those days – and it finished with all the young kids sitting on the mounds of straw which had been pushed back into high piles. It was a bizarre sight, with all these youngsters sitting on top of these straw mounds, but the worst that happened, thankfully, was just a few kids in tears.

The third game, at Hull City, again saw us level 1–1 after 90 minutes and it appeared that absolutely nothing was going to separate us. Something would, though. In the discussions leading up to extra time Don said out of the blue: 'If anybody gets anywhere near the box, get down.' Jimmy Greenhoff, who was quick when he was in full flight, set off on one of his jinking runs and was fully five yards outside the penalty area when he was brought down. By the time he had stumbled, fallen and rolled over a couple of times he was inside the box and the referee, Jim Finney, pointed to the spot so quickly that it was almost embarrassing. Not only did he award the penalty, he also sent off George Mulhall and George Hurd, two of Sunderland's Scottish players, for protesting. This was at a time when there was a lot of talk about referees being got at. I am not saying that Finney was, but the issue begged close examination. Firstly, why did Revie issue that 'dive' instruction and, secondly, why did Finney award a penalty that so clearly was not? Lots of things were happening in football that simply did not add up, and this was just another of those. In any event, Johnny Giles converted the penalty and we were through to the quarter-finals. Mulhall is to this day quite irate about the situation. The Sunderland old boys are 100 per cent sure that that was not a straight game. As players, you never know. You get feelings about certain things when you are out there on the pitch, and I remember thinking in the dressing-room after that game, 'That was a funny statement of Don's.' Maybe he thought that Jim had not so far given a penalty and might do so at the next debatable incident, maybe there were other factors.

Whatever, it was that incident which made me realise that I was in the seething cauldron of the big time. This was no amateur stuff. It was big money; high stakes. And further it was a wake-up call for me about the world in which I was now inhabiting. No longer was I a young, naive kid with stars in his eyes. We beat Manchester City in the next round and went on to that further controversial meeting with Chelsea, and the injustice of the 1–0 defeat, but at the end of the season I had become aware of an emerging pattern. Many people were asking why this fabulous Leeds side did not win more trophies and although the question was not easy to answer then it certainly is in retrospect. Our bogey was that Don wanted to win everything. We were competing on all fronts: the league, two domestic cup competitions and Europe, and really it was impossible.

The passage of time has shown that it pays dividends to set out your stall to win just one of these and revel in the glory of success on any plateau. But that was not Don. He was so ambitious at the time that he wanted to win literally everything. Granted, he was so far ahead in his thinking, but what he did not realise was that there is a limit to the number of games individuals and teams can play. One season we played 76 games and that is an incredible number. What he should have done was to prioritise; set his stall out for the league one year and a European trophy the next.

Another thing about Don was that he liked to brag about the great squad he had while never really believing in them. He had good players like Mick Bates, Rod Belfitt, Terry Hibbitt and Terry Yorath, but he had fixed in his mind a first eleven of which they were not really a part. There was many a game in which people had injuries or needed resting but, like everything else, he had the club doctors in his pocket. He ruled everybody. There would be three players on the treatment tables and as the doc was going round their legs he would glance up to Don, whose nod meant that he was going to play and whose shake of the head would mean that the player was going to be dropped whatever the doctor's opinion.

Don ran the place. His word was law. There came about a huge clash between him and the chairman, Harry Reynolds, and the upshot was that it was Reynolds, not Don, who left. He had become so powerful. Every season there were new rumours about him leaving Leeds to join this club or that, and it has always been my feeling that this was just to put extra pressure on Leeds to increase his wage packet. Don always said that he was going to retire in his early fifties and enjoy life, and this of course required the amassing of money. He also knew how to use the press. If he thought it would do him any good he would not be averse to stories that he was wanted elsewhere, thereby raising his stock at Leeds United. Conversely, if anybody wrote in derogatory terms about his team he would tell the paper responsible not to bother sending its representative to the next game because he would not be allowed in. And he meant it.

He was a manoeuvrer, manipulator and planner. He was also the worst loser on the planet. I have never known a man take defeat so badly, so personally, and this was a weakness of his. After a defeat he would send in the same eleven for the next game, with the idea that reputations had to be redeemed, rather than improvising with his squad. Instead of focusing on winning the league, if we had a chance, he would ask players to perform consecutively in a European game, a league game and a domestic cup game rather than resting a few. Every game to him, no matter what its value or significance, was life or death.

But despite our relative success that season we scored surprisingly few goals. Johnny Giles was top scorer with 18; I bagged 13 in 39 games. Our reputation was such that if we went a goal up then that was the end of the game. We were being encouraged by Don to shut up shop after we had scored and a win-at-all-costs mentality was adopted. We were not liked for this, but nobody inside the club cared about that. Although the crowds were always good, between 35,000 and 45,000, entertainment was not a priority. Winning was.

Gillian and I were married on Grand National day in 1969. All the family came down from Scotland and they had no problem in picking the appropriately named big-race winner, Highland Wedding, at the rewarding odds of 100–9. We went off to the west coast of Scotland on honeymoon, stopping off at Berwick on the way, but it turned out to be something of a disaster because my new wife was soon laid low with flu. I had to tell our hotelier in Fort William that the honeymoon would have to be cut short and we headed back on the long drive south.

I had bought a nice semi-detached house (33 The Grove, Alwoodley) from the club for £2,400 and we quickly settled in to domestic bliss.

chapter five

CARELESS HANDS

GOING INTO THE 1967–68 SEASON DON DECIDED TO CHANGE HIS STRATEGY
a little. In the previous two campaigns we had not been getting
enough goals from the main strikers. The supply had dried up a bit.
I had got 13, Jimmy Greenhoff scored 12, Rod Belfitt 9 and Johnny
Giles was our leading scorer with 18 from midfield. We needed a
centre-forward in the old-fashioned mould and Don went out and
bought one of the great journeymen players who would work his
socks off and get you goals in Mick Jones from Sheffield United for
£100,000. Mick had been scoring loads of goals over at Bramall Lane
and his arrival on the scene, albeit not right at the start of the season,
acted as a spur to everyone in the side with goalscoring ambitions,
not least me. This was the first time I hit the 30-goal mark, while
Greenhoff scored 16, in a season notable once again for the high
number of games we played. The season ran to 64 matches because,
again, we had another bumper campaign. It had started with high
expectations that we might win all four competitions in which we
were competing, the League, FA Cup, League Cup and Inter Cities,
and with two months remaining we were well on course to fulfil these
lofty ambitions. We topped the league, got to the semi-final of the FA
Cup against Everton and still had chances in the other two.

But for me this was the point at which our goalkeeper, Gary Sprake, lost his nerve. He started to feel the pressure in the big games, which were really getting to him, and in the FA Cup run alone he took it upon himself to start lashing out at any player who upset him. Players, of course, cottoned on to this. I was the back-up goalkeeper and in the fifth round against Bristol City at Elland Road I finished up between the sticks after Gary had swung a punch at their centre-forward and, of course, got sent off. Despite this we won the game as everybody might have expected. By now, though, Gary's suspect temperament was folklore in the game and come the semi-final big Joe Royle, Everton's rampaging centre-forward, started to eyeball and hustle him. Gary couldn't take it. His task in booting the ball upfield was simple enough, but he fluffed it completely and sent it just a short distance to Jimmy Husband, who chipped it back towards the open goal. Jack Charlton was forced to handle the ball, which was going in – that offence today would have meant his instant dismissal – and the resulting penalty saw our dismissal from the competition. It was a game we should have won because we were better than Everton, despite the inclusion in their side of such illustrious names as Alan Ball, Howard Kendall and Colin Harvey.

This was a bitter blow to us, although we did win the League Cup. The semi-final was over two legs against Derby County, managed then by the mercurial Brian Clough. We won the first leg at the Baseball Ground by a single goal and reached the final with a 3–2 success in the return at Elland Road, fuelling, in the process, Clough's hatred of Leeds United.

It happened that this year I was the winner of the national Sports Personality of the Year award, held at the Queen's Hotel, Leeds, and screened by Yorkshire Television who ran it in conjunction with the Variety Club. It was not necessarily a Yorkshireman who would win this – Formula One's Jackie Stewart had been a previous choice – but could be any individual voted for by the viewers. Having scored 30 goals in a side which had had such a good season clearly swung it my way, but unfortunately Mr Clough had been chosen as the guest speaker at a packed-out ceremony which came hot on the heels of those semi-finals. I was presented with the award by the Prime Minister of the time, Harold Wilson, and within moments Clough was on his feet. He said: 'Right. I have had to listen to a load of crap for the last hour. I'm bursting for a pee, so you can all sit there and wait.' This was notwithstanding the presence of the most important man in the country, a host of civic dignitaries, directors of the club and sundry other esteemed guests. What followed on Clough's return from relieving himself was a searing attack on me personally and on Leeds United in general.

Revie's strict rules dictated that because we had a match 48 hours after this event I was to leave as soon as I had picked up my award, so after I had acknowledged the people and said my thank-yous I was on my way. From early the next morning I was besieged by telephone calls relating what had been said in my absence. The theme of Clough's speech was that the award I had won was meant to be for sportsmen, when all I did was dive. Clearly still seething from that semi-final reverse, and even more transparently very drunk, Clough was booed off the stage after no more than three or four minutes and was forced to sit down. The Prime Minister, a Yorkshireman himself, had stated his delight that Leeds United were putting the county back on the map after a fallow period and had spoken very well, so quite what he made of his company on the podium is anybody's guess.

Clough's outburst, I have to say, did not worry me in the least. What an opposing manager had to say was the last thing on your mind. I had always greatly admired him previously and that admiration has been undiminished since, because his managerial achievements bordered on the unbelievable. But as the years went by, and the more successful we became – although they pipped us for the league championship a bit later on – his passionate hatred of Leeds United and Don Revie was self-evident. The criticism he levelled at me may, in hindsight, have been justified. In the first minute of the League Cup final against Arsenal, which we won 1–0 courtesy of a goal by Terry Cooper, Bob McNab gave an insight into the orders he had been given when he put me right up in the air as I put the ball past him and tried to run on. I would have been singled out as a potential dangerman and the instructions to defenders in those days were to seize the first opportunity that came their way to 'Give 'em what for'.

He caught me, but I made it look bad. He was booked. To my thinking, it was a way of getting protection from referees. If you didn't let them know, the officials would think: 'Oh, he's all right. Let him get on with it.' I got up and said to Bob: 'Excuse me, that's you fucked now. You've hit me and got a card straightaway, so you've got 89 minutes of the game to go and you can't hit me again.'

Straightaway the ball was in my court. It was professionalism. When I see players overreacting now, it's often for nothing, with people pretending they have been elbowed. I would do it, probably a little bit more than I should have, only when a player had actually gone for me and could have inflicted an injury. In certain circumstances when you've had a clatter it does you good to stay down and get the trainer on. That means everybody is going to take notice of what is happening and you do get a bit more protection than if you had just got up and got on with the game.

The League Cup was our first domestic trophy, won at Wembley and held aloft in front of a crowd of 97,000 by our captain Billy Bremner. For three successive nights before this big match Terry Cooper dreamed that he would score the winning goal, and proof that dreams can come true came when our left-back did just that after 17 minutes. Eddie Gray sent over one of his specials from the corner flag, and when George Graham's clearing header from under the bar reached him at the edge of the box Terry lashed a brilliant volley into the roof of the net. You remember things like that. It was all the more sweet for us having been beaten in two European finals by Real Zaragoza and Dynamo Zagreb. We'd been runners-up, then fourth, in the league and we had gone close in the cup competitions. Your first trophy is the hardest to come by and it was a great day for us, followed by a reception at which thousands of fans cheered their hearts out as the cup was displayed on the steps of the Town Hall.

This being in March, there were two months of the season remaining and we were still going for the FA Cup, although we lost in the semis, were still in the Fairs Cup, which we went on to win, and still on course for the championship. The great disappointment was the way in which we fell away in the league. Although only five points separated the top four teams we had to be content with fourth position, having lost our last four games on the bounce. The league was won by a very good Manchester City side captained by Tony Book and featuring a tremendous forward line in Mike Summerbee, Francis Lee, Neil Young, Colin Bell and Tony Coleman. It was the team that all City fans talk about now. Lots of people had backed us to win all four competitions and the fact that there was general disappointment that we won two spoke volumes for the expectancy level associated with this team. In the FA Cup final Everton were beaten by West Brom, 1–0 after extra time, with all the best teams having gone out, and that had to be looked upon as a missed opportunity. Only the sheer number of games could be the explanation for our falling away in the league at such a critical time, but we were to pick up our second trophy in a European final which was put back to the beginning of the following season because of fixture congestion.

This was the Fairs Cup double-header against Ferencvaros in which Gary Sprake won back his colours. We won 1–0 at Elland Road, but in those days, unlike now, Hungarian football was very strong and travelling there was a daunting prospect. The match in Budapest attracted a crowd of 76,000, but we shut up shop and, backed up by a brilliant performance from Gary, we finished 0–0. Without question Gary cost us a few trophies, but this was one occasion when he could have been said to have won it for us. Of course, making good saves was what he was there for in the first place.

I particularly enjoyed the Fairs Cup run that season. In the three rounds leading to the final we played Hibernian, Rangers and Dundee and, being from Scotland, this was a bit special. I managed to see my family on each of these trips north of the border and they went to all of the games. This was the first time I had played against the famous Glasgow Rangers, something I had always wanted to do, and it was fairly straightforward for us, drawing 0–0 up there and beating them 2–0 at Elland Road. We thought Dundee, then, would be a formality in the semi-final, but it was 1–1 at Dundee, with Paul Madeley getting one of his rare goals, and when the return was played at Elland Road we had all hell on our hands. We scraped through 1–0 by virtue of a goal from Eddie Gray and one of the reasons that we struggled so much was that the old Kop, now the Revie Stand, was in the process of being pulled down so that behind the goal was like a building site. Full house in the absence of this stand was 23,000 and there was just no atmosphere. In our FA Cup run there had been 48,000 and 45,000 against Bristol City and Sheffield United.

It had been a really big season, yet Don was not happy. Bitterly disappointed about the way in which our championship challenge had faded away, he could not see that he was partly to blame. He had played the same team in far too many matches. Bodies have only so much to give and we had given our all. Throughout the season Don had been a bit grumpy. There were strong rumours month by month that he was about to leave Elland Road, with Sunderland supposedly the club to which he was going. We were aware of this speculation, though we did not know how much significance should be attached to it. Although he was a great manager, and loved us all, Don was always alert to the question of his financial security. He never did go to Sunderland, though later in his career he made lots of moves to better himself on the money front. He always said that he wanted to retire at the age of 54 and go on and enjoy life, playing golf and pursuing other hobbies and interests. Whether he used offers from other clubs to get Leeds to improve his deal I don't know, but certainly there was a black cloud over the club at the back end of the season.

Background debate was raging as to who would take over if he were to leave. There was nobody among the players at the club – we were all too young – and it was difficult to imagine to whom the chairman Harry Reynolds would turn outside the club for a replacement. As it was, we were to go into the 1968–69 season with the status quo intact and with an air of invincibility about us. The problem with that, as Manchester United have discovered since the formation of the Premiership, is that every game played against the smaller teams was like a cup final for the opposition. Teams like Stoke City would build themselves up for a visit by Leeds, knowing that the game would be played in front of a bumper crowd, television coverage was likely and somebody might make a name for himself.

We won the First Division championship that season for the first time in the club's history and it may have been no coincidence that this came about because of early exits from the League Cup and the FA Cup and a casual attitude towards the Fairs Cup. We were knocked out of the League Cup by Crystal Palace in October and out of the FA Cup by Sheffield Wednesday in early January, so that we had fully four months in which to concentrate our efforts on the league in a season which amounted to 55 games, 10 or so less than had become the norm. In recent years John Giles and myself have had many conversations about the old days and we agree that although we probably should have won more than we did, we were prevented from doing so by Don's blind ambition. He wanted to win everything.

Right from the word go we had a hammer-and-tongs battle with Liverpool for the title. We could not have made a better start, winning seven and drawing two of our first nine games, and in Europe, viewed as a welcome relief from the pressures of the league, Don started to use his squad a bit more. After beating Hanover, Naples and Standard Liege we went out 3–0 on aggregate to Ujpest Dosza.

With Mick Jones nicely settled in the side – he finished top scorer with 17 while I hit 13 – our pursuit of the championship became obsessive. The pressure in the dressing-room became more intense with each passing game and had become almost unbearable by the time we went to Anfield for what would be the championship decider against Liverpool. I was injured and had to sit it out, although I travelled, and when the match finished 0–0 the crowded Kop regaled us with what seemed a never-ending chorus of 'Champions' which was eventually to go right round the stadium. That from home supporters for an away side which had just deprived them of the title! As our players made their way off Don said to Billy: 'Have you heard that?' and the lads went back to the Kop to salute them. This spoke volumes for Liverpool Football Club and their fans. They were then, and always have been, a credit to the game. To this day there has been a lot of respect between Leeds and Liverpool and I believe it goes back to that occasion. Both teams have spent so many years challenging each other for honours and the games between them are always played in a great spirit.

Our final game of the season saw us beat Nottingham Forest 1–0 at Elland Road in front of 46,000 – and it was party time! Don always liked us to go back to the Queen's Hotel and have a sing-song, although the lads were always less than enthusiastic about having to take centre stage. Don's love of singing probably came from his wife Elsie, who would have been brought up on the Scottish house parties in which all individuals are expected to give a rendition. If Don said you had to get up you got up. If you weren't very good you were allowed a singing partner and I would always trill, accompanied by one of the girls, that old Frank and Nancy Sinatra song 'Something Stupid'. All the lads had their party piece. Mick Jones would take off Elvis Presley and by the time Billy rose to sing 'I Left My Heart In San Francisco' with his lovely wife Vicky he was usually too pissed to remember the words. We wanted to get off into town and have a few drinks, so that by the time we got back it was way past the boss's bedtime and he had retired, thankfully having left the champagne on ice for us. Two or three sherries and Don had had enough. His staff were just the same. The next morning at Elland Road was fabulous, with all the media trying to get interviews with players who were still pissed from the night before. The party went on for three days and a civic reception followed, when the city had had time to organise it.

All the players were now getting recognition and Leeds had internationals right through their squad. There was a total of 16 players representing their various countries and Mick O'Grady, who became a great pal of mine, was perhaps the biggest surprise of these. He had the most amazing record. Playing twice for England, he scored in both games yet was never picked again. We called him Shady O'Grady, because he was something of a ladies' man and would be very secretive about what he was doing. He was always speaking in hushed tones on the telephone and was a perpetual ducker and diver, never letting anybody know what he was up to.

Mick Jones wasn't the sharpest tool in the box and his nickname was Muttley, after the cartoon dog whose mouth was always open in a gormless way. Every day after training Gilesy would take Mick's towel into the showers and stand on it in all the mucky water, leaving him with an uncomfortable drying-off exercise. But instead of determining to hide his towel the next day so that it would remain clean and fresh, Mick would fall for it every time.

Don had taken us to Scarborough for one of his favoured three-day breaks aimed at fostering team spirit and I was in a bar talking to two girls when Mick walked in. I thought I had better introduce him and said: 'Mick, this is Barbara and this is Joan.'

I told him that Joan had been in training and was about to swim the Channel. 'What, from here?' was his studied response. As he sidled away the look on the girl's face was as if to say: 'Is he thick or something?' That was Mick. But what a player.

These breaks were typical of Don's thinking. He never wanted us to be at home. He wanted his squad to be together all the time and even before home games we would be ordered to meet at the Craiglands Hotel in Ilkley. We had two nights, three at the most, at home. We would have a situation where we would play on the Saturday, go home for a night out with your wife, but report to the Craiglands on Sunday lunchtime and remain there until the game at

Elland Road on Wednesday night. It was difficult keeping your mind occupied, and Don's solution was to introduce carpet bowls and bingo. His reasoning for our spending four or five nights a week in hotels was that many of the squad had young children, giving rise to the possibility that we would not get sufficient sleep.

In those days I used to love playing darts and dominoes in the Wetherby League. I would go up to the George and Dragon, where all the racing crowd congregated, and we would have a real good games night over a few pints, often until one o'clock in the morning or later, if there was no midweek game. It was a great way of letting your hair down. Players of that era were far more sociable and of a more workaday mentality than is the case today. We would have a couple of drinks with the locals, who would just treat us as one of their number. That's why, I believe, the players were so popular in the city. We were part of the city. Billy and Jack used to go in The Woodman at Halton and they, too, loved their games of dominoes. Today's players tend to lock themselves away in their ivory towers, thinking of themselves in the movie star bracket and that is down to the money they are earning rather than whatever measure of success they are achieving. We, as champions of England, loved getting out and about and mixing with the people while the current crop, without having won anything or done anything in the game, seem to think they are above all that.

Of course they are all millionaires and people in that bracket tend to change from what they once were. We never forgot where we came from. Billy would sometimes get a bit pissed and aggressive; I have always been at home among ordinary working people and never more so than when I went back home to Scotland among my old pals. It wasn't like the prodigal son returning with a personality changed by success. We were normal people doing normal things like going into town, going to a pub, going to a club and all, of course, within the bounds of the football club rules. Nobody was allowed to be seen in a pub less than 48 hours before a game, and though we would have a good drink when we could, nobody abused the situation.

Maybe the press is to blame for the current attitude. When I was playing, journalists were your biggest drinking pals. Every pressman had every player's telephone number in his contact book, and if they wanted to know something quickly they were quite at liberty to ring any of us at home. Naturally all our squad members were big targets for lots of other clubs, so that transfer rumours were flying about all the time. Don would often say that there was a pile of offers on his desk, but the fact was that none of us wanted to go anywhere. We were already with the best team. Certainly we could have gone for more money, but where could we have gone for more trophies? The Italian and Spanish markets were not open in those days because their domestic game had declined so markedly. In much the same way as we have too many foreign players in Britain now, they had a surfeit of imports and decided to ban them for a period of about six years.

Every other team would have wanted to buy any one of us, God knows at what kind of figure translated to the modern market. You couldn't put a price on their heads. People ask what I would have been worth now and I can only tell them if you're a wide player and you score 30 goals in a season then you'd better start counting the noughts! David Beckham's a wide player and if he gets a dozen he's had a wonderful season.

I was earning £160 a week. Having been part of a title-winning team I became utterly determined to have that hiked up to £200 but it proved a more elusive target than I had bargained for. Don lived just round the corner from me and in the close season he rang me three times to go round to talk turkey. 'You've got £190,' he told me. 'No, I'm not signing for anything under £200,' I said. In the final analysis, the day before the season started, I was round again at his request. 'This is my final offer,' said Don. 'You're getting £196 a week.' I told him: 'It has to be £200.'

That evening I went to talk to my Turkish brother-in-law, Toosh, a restaurateur in Leeds, and told him how the negotiations had proceeded. 'Don't you see?' he said. 'All it is, is that he does not want you to get your own way. He wants to show who's boss. Paying you what you demanded would mean that he had weakened in the eyes of the players.' When he pointed out that after tax on the £4 difference we were talking about I would be less than £2 better off there seemed no point in pursuing it any further.

The tax rate then was between 50 and 60 per cent and many of us players were lucky that Gilesy was involved in the insurance business with a partner, Sean Skeen, who had gone to the Government with a proposal that footballers should be allowed to draw their pension at the age of 35 as that was seen to be the end of their careers. They agreed to that. Say, with bonuses, I earned £17,000 a year then £8,500 of that would have gone to the Government. But we were allowed to put up to a third of our wages into the pension scheme and nowadays, before I start on any other kind of work, I draw £210 a week from my old index-linked pension. It's a help; a bit of a start on the average wage-earner. And we have Johnny to thank for that. Not only was he the brains on the field, he was the wise one off it, too.

The money we were earning was probably double that of some other big clubs like Manchester United. That was the reason that Rangers and Celtic lost all their good players like Lou Macari and Kenny Dalglish to England. Their view was that you should play for them for the honour, not the money. It was the big-club attitude to footballers, and it is quite significant that the reverse is now the norm. When directors start screaming now, I think: 'Well, you had it coming.' When they signed you they owned you for life. They could put you out of the game if they so desired and you had no comeback. When our great team split up a few years down the line the directors still insisted on getting a paltry £40,000 for you instead of saying: 'There you are. After all those great years of service, it's the least you deserve.'

In our championship-winning season, when we were attracting crowds of 38,000–45,000, the lads all got together and urged Billy to go to see the manager about the possibility of our being paid a crowd bonus. Our existing bonuses were difficult enough to achieve. The win bonus was £80 – but only if we were top of the league. Otherwise it was scaled down and you had to be in the top three to get any bonus at all other than the £20 minimum. The offer was: 30,000–35,000 an extra £2 per thousand; 35,000 upwards an extra £5 per thousand – but only if we won. Less tax.

No player ever made enough money out of football to be able to retire in comfort. Right up until England won the World Cup, Jack Charlton lived in one of the modest semi-detached houses opposite Elland Road. But, let's face it, a semi-detached house was very swish to somebody who had come from a council estate, and mansions were for true celebrities. You needed every penny you could lay your hands on and Jack was always very cash conscious. There was no club shop and Jack obtained permission from the club to sell merchandise like hats, scarves and badges from three trailers stationed around the ground. He would tow them down to the ground on the back of his car from his house and in no time business was thriving. His lovely wife Pat never got to see a game – she was busy organising the selling and collecting the money, and they made an awful lot of money out of this enterprise. In the end, when the club realised the revenue they were missing out on and wanted to take control themselves, they had to come to some arrangement with Jack because he had a verbal agreement with the chairman.

If anybody deserved every penny of what he got it was Jack; great clubman, great player, great guy. His career, both as a player and as a manager, was quite extraordinary. He was at Leeds for more than 20 years, making no fewer than 773 appearances and scoring 96 goals, which is a phenomenal haul for a centre-half. He had to wait until shortly before his 30th birthday before collecting his first England cap in 1965, yet within 18 months he became the proud owner of a World Cup winner's medal. And in 1967 he was voted Footballer of the Year. He had managed Middlesbrough, Sheffield Wednesday and Newcastle before his celebrated link-up with the Republic of Ireland, whom he took to the quarter-finals of the World Cup in 1990 and the last 16 in 1994. He's the biggest leprechaun I've ever seen!

chapter six

PIMPLES AND SANDPAPER

DEFENDING CHAMPIONS. THIS WAS PRECISELY WHAT DON REVIE HAD IN MIND when, having taken over from Jack Taylor in 1961, almost the first thing he did was to change the Leeds United strip from its traditional blue and gold to the all-white of Real Madrid. The European Cup final of 1960 produced what has always been regarded as the best club match ever played when the Spaniards, di Stefano, Puskas et al, pulverised Eintracht Frankfurt 7–3 in front of 127,000 astonished onlookers at Hampden. And in Don's eyes if you wanted to be the best you had to look like the best. For a side in Division Two and looking like it might be relegated to Division Three, such lofty heights could, to an outsider, have constituted only pipe dreams. Yet here we were, less than a decade down the line from when he assumed control, with Don's dream fulfilled.

Strikingly, each passing season saw a new team emerge to challenge for honours alongside us. First it was Liverpool, then Manchester United, then Manchester City, followed by the Ball–Kendall–Harvey Everton. Season 1969–70 saw Everton steal our crown and over the next two years Arsenal and Derby County came out of the pack. The one constant when it came to being in contention for everything was ourselves, the young pack of lads who had come through under Don's watchful gaze. Just every now and then, like the Busby Babes and the current crop at Leeds United who reached European semi-finals in consecutive seasons at the turn of the millennium, you get an exceptional set of youngsters emerging together, putting their clubs on a solid footing for many years.

Now he had won a league title, the European Cup topped Don's agenda. We sent out a warning of this intent in the first round with a resounding 10–0 first-leg defeat of the Norwegians Lyn (Oslo) over there – that remains the club's record cup victory – and a 6–0 thrashing in the second leg. We had been joined at Elland Road in the close season by Allan Clarke, unquestionably an upmarket player, but a funny lad in many ways. One of five Staffordshire-born footballing brothers, he was very unpopular in the game. When you played against him there was no way you could like him. He was a bit snidey; a trampler of ankles and always with an elbow at the ready. Yet for me, as a wide player, his addition to the team was fantastic. I now had the choice of Jones at the far post and Clarke at the near post and so empathetic did our playing together become that I didn't even have to look up before crossing the ball. I knew when I was going up the wing, depending upon the room I had or the situation I was in, exactly where the pair would be at any split second in time. We were a terrific threesome, and in this season we scored between us no fewer than 71 goals – Jones and Clarke 26 apiece and myself 19. When you add into that mix Johnny Giles' 19, Billy Bremner's 16 and Eddie Gray's 10 it shows how potent a force we had become. Boring Leeds? Do me a favour. We finished the season with 84 league goals while Arsenal, the champions, netted 72. We were always being tagged 'Boring Leeds' or 'Dirty Leeds' and the only reason was that so few teams enjoyed success against us. It was jealousy.

Sniffer Clarke joined us from Leicester for a then British record transfer fee of £165,000, having first come to prominence at Fulham, with the reputation of being selfish. There were rumours from the 1969 FA Cup final, when Leicester went down to Manchester City by the only goal of the game, that he would not be a part of the players' pool which is traditionally formed for paid media interviews ahead of the big occasion, the proceeds being shared out equally among the squad. He saw himself as the star of the show and wanted to go it alone. When he came to Leeds it was evident that he was an arrogant lad, but in his arrogance was his confidence in himself. He had an amazing self-belief in his ability to score goals. Although we found him to be a smashing lad, you could understand why he was so widely disliked. Sniffer, who scored 151 goals in 366 appearances for Leeds, once had the audacity to go out against Liverpool with a little piece of sandpaper tucked in his shorts pocket. His marker that day was the ultra-tough Tommy Smith, whose complexion could most kindly be described as pimply and most rudely as pock-marked. We asked Sniffer what the sandpaper was for and he replied that he was going to give it to Smith at the end of the match so that he could rub away his spots, and that he was going to tell him so beforehand.

As soon as we ran out Sniffer was true to his word. 'Here you are, Tommy,' he said. 'A present for you. When you're having a bath after the game, this will help get rid of all those spots.' He was a brave lad. Of course, Tommy spent the entire match chasing Sniffer all over the park, but we were to learn subsequently that if the Liverpool legend didn't like Clarke then there was an individual in his own ranks whom he hated even more. During a visit to Anfield Clarkey, who really relished winding up and goading opponents, was a bit naughty in a challenge with Emlyn Hughes. As they went up for a ball, Clarkey smashed his elbow into Hughes' face and instantly there was blood everywhere. This led to a real mêlée towards which Smith ran 40 yards to get involved. Billy Bremner put his hand across his opponent and said: 'Hey, Tommy, you keep out of this. It's nothing to do with you.'

Smith peered down at a heavily bleeding and screaming Hughes and said: 'You know, Billy, I think I could get to like that Allan Clarke!' That was another incident in which an underlying mutual respect between Leeds and Liverpool was evident. They were a fine side and we were developing into one of the best club sides that England has ever produced. Unfortunately we never won as much silverware as we should have done, but to win the league or be second, and get to domestic and European finals on a regular basis over a period spanning a dozen years or so, was a hell of an achievement, particularly when you consider the number of matches we played basically with the same squad. Jones and Clarke had joined the nucleus of Sprake, Reaney, Cooper, Bremner, Charlton, Hunter, Giles, Lorimer and Gray and we were household names. Still to this day the fans of that era trip the names off the tongue in a way that they cannot do even with modern-day Manchester United. With Sunderland and Leicester they'd give you three or four names.

Don's dreams of European Cup glory were dashed as once again we ran into a fixture pile-up, this time of astronomical proportions. The luck of the draw in the FA Cup was with us right until the semi-finals, when we ended up playing three games against Manchester United, having beaten Swansea, Sutton United, Mansfield and Swindon. This trio of games for the right to play in the Cup final saw us first draw 0–0 at Sheffield, then 0–0 at Villa Park and eventually win 1–0 at Bolton with Billy scoring the all-important goal. But these games became entangled with the two legs of the European Cup semi-final against Celtic and three league matches in an unbelievable sequence which saw us play eight matches in a fortnight.

Don, it should be explained, had fallen out with the Football League secretary Alan Hardaker. He would swing the lead if he thought it necessary and the nationwide flu epidemic, which was doing the rounds at this critical time, appeared to the boss to be the ideal opportunity to seek the postponement of some of these games. Dispensation had been given to some clubs whose squads had been decimated to call off matches and Don sought to jump on the bandwagon. It worked once, but these two powerful figures crossed swords when Don pleaded sickness a second time. This, I feel, worked against Leeds in subsequent years, for the FA were never very accommodating when a problem affecting the club was put before them. Had they seen eye to eye I am sure the FA would have looked at a situation demanding eight games in fourteen days and taken some helpful action. But they did nothing other than to make us play on relentlessly. I can, to an extent, understand the FA stance. We were the first team, playing upwards of 70 games a season, to present them with such a problem and they did not really know how to handle it. There was also the matter of the domestic season having to get finished on time because of the World Cup in Mexico. But to ask a club to play so many games in so few days was criminal, really. They start screaming now at four games in a fortnight.

Celtic's Lisbon Lions – so-called because of their stirring victory over Inter Milan in the European Cup final of 1967 – were a great side, featuring Jimmy Johnstone and Bobby Murdoch, but we had played them twice in prestige matches and beaten them and there was no reason other than fatigue that should have prevented us from beating them over two legs here. Such was their domination in Scotland that they could get away with fielding four or five regular players in league games and keep the remainder for their European exploits. We, meanwhile, were playing three semi-finals, league games and facing them in a European semi-final.

We had two fantastic matches against Celtic. With an early goal by George Connelly they beat us 1–0 at Elland Road and the return attracted an all-time British record crowd of 136,505. And that was just those who paid to get in! I was led to believe that untold numbers of people got in free under the turnstiles or over the walls, so goodness knows what the real crowd was. Billy scored an absolute peach of a goal in the first ten minutes to level matters, but unfortunately all that did was raise false hopes. Tiredness bordering on exhaustion – my own legs felt very heavy – ensured that we never reached the performance levels of which we were capable. We gave it our best shot, but Gary Sprake went off injured to be replaced by David Harvey, whose first job was to pick their equaliser on the night, and the tie's winning goal, out of the back of the net.

In the 1970 FA Cup final at Wembley, sandwiched between those two Celtic clashes, our opponents were Chelsea. For some lunatic reason that year it was decided to hold the Horse of the Year Show on the football pitch at Wembley instead of its usual venue, Olympia. There was torrential rain and, of course, the pitch was just like a quagmire come kick-off time. The horses had damaged all the drains and the area to the right of the royal box was awash with surface water, giving Wembley the kind of mudbath appearance which had never been seen before. Nonetheless, Eddie Gray proceeded to give David Webb such a chasing as we played so well that, with a Jack Charlton goal under our belts, we were cruising. Until, that is, Gary Sprake proceeded to have a disastrous moment. Right on the stroke of half-time Peter Houseman hit a shot from 30 yards which bounced three times before squirting under our keeper's body.

We came out for the second half with all guns blazing and such was our domination that it had to be the most one-sided final of all time. With six minutes left, Mick Jones scored what just had to be the winning goal. But we reckoned without Gary. Another long-range ball went into the box and instead of just leaving it alone he went to kick it away, totally mishit it and it fell to John Hollins. We weren't ready for the Hollins cross, which Ian Hutchinson headed home.

Another match was just what we did not need, with our prevailing fixture schedule and the second leg against Celtic so close, yet we now faced a Cup final replay – the first since 1912 – at Old Trafford. This was the proverbial game of two halves. A first-half Mick Jones goal put us in the driving seat, but in the second half Chelsea changed their tactics, moving David Webb into the middle to get him away from Gray and putting Ron Harris on him instead. Harris fully lived up to his nickname 'Chopper', mercilessly hacking away at our most potent attacking force on the day and in the process stifling our movement. They reaped a big dividend, equalising 12 minutes from time through Peter Osgood, and scoring again a minute before the extra-time interval through Webb, of all people, to take the coveted trophy. From mid-March we had been a hot tip to win the treble, but on the run-in our league form stuttered badly. We lost to teams like Southampton, Derby, Manchester City and Ipswich and, in fact, won only one of our last six games. We finished with nothing – second in the league, runners-up in the FA Cup and semi-finalists in the European Cup. To the average fan that would represent a great season, but for us it was a heartbreaker. With expectations having been so high, the fact that there was no silverware to put into the Elland Road trophy cabinet made everybody really depressed.

It was not a happy close-season and when the action resumed in season 1970–71 Arsenal, who had finished only 12th the previous season, emerged as the big force. We were hammer and tongs all season, with the two of us drawing 13 points clear of the rest and the Londoners eventually pipping us by a single point, 65–64. The record books show that 64 points, with two points for a win, was always enough to win the championship, but on this occasion the trend was bucked. The key figure in their success, amazingly, was their goalkeeper Bob Wilson, whom previously nobody had ever rated.

Our fourth last game in the run-in was a highly controversial clash with West Bromwich Albion at Elland Road. I was injured and listened to the match on the radio at home, but the overwhelming unfairness of what happened came streaming over the airwaves. Albion were already a goal up when, 20 minutes into the second half, Tony Brown dispossessed Norman Hunter and followed the ball as it rebounded into our half. One of their players was flagged offside near the centre circle but the referee, Ray Tinkler, ignored this and waved play on. Further, Brown released the ball to an even more evidently offside Jeff Astle, who went on to score. All hell broke loose. Our fans invaded the pitch, causing a five-minute delay, and unfortunately a linesman was hit on the head with a stone. Albion went on to win 2–1, their first away win for 16 months, and nobody connected with Leeds will hear anything other than it being the ref's shocking decision which cost us the title. To be fair to the West Brom lads, they were saddened to have won a match in such a way.

We won our last three games and although Arsenal had a couple of games in hand the requirement was for them to take ten points from five games. Nobody expected them to do it – but they did. Don did his best to prevent them from doing so. Their last match, the one which would decide the destiny of the title, was against their arch-enemies Tottenham Hotspur at White Hart Lane, and in the knowledge that Spurs would do no favours at all for their north London rivals, Don dispatched his loyal friend Herbert Warner, a local jeweller, to White Hart Lane a couple of days before the game with an extra 'incentive'. There was nothing wrong with this; it was merely a little present for each of them if they should beat Arsenal. Despite giving everything, they did not beat them, and all credit to Arsenal, who won in the most dramatic fashion with a headed Ray Kennedy goal two minutes from time.

This season, 1970–71, also featured what was probably the club's worst ever humiliation. It came about in the FA Cup. We beat Swindon 4–0 away in the fourth round on the day that my son Simon was born – I had special dispensation to miss the match because of the impending family event – but in the next round, as leaders of the First Division, we were drawn away to Fourth Division Colchester United. They had big Ray Crawford, the former Ipswich and England centre-forward, playing for them and although he was on his way down he was too smart a cookie for Sprake. Crawford was a big, strong lad who ten years previously had topped the First Division goalscoring chart and Gary just bottled it as the striker scored twice to give them a comfortable 2–0 half-time lead. They were three up after 55 minutes and although we pulled it back to 3–2 the bird had flown. Gary had played so well for us early in his career, but it is no understatement to say that he became an embarrassment. He lost the plot and began to let us down on a regular basis, costing us matches all over the place. Despite this, Don persisted in playing him. Whether it was a lack of confidence in David Harvey, or that he did not think he was ready, I don't know. But Gary had completely gone.

We did win the Fairs Cup. After such difficult early-round treks to the likes of Dynamo Dresden we faced a humdinger semi-final pairing with the old enemy, Liverpool. Two fabulous contests were decided by a single Billy Bremner goal and we were into our third Fairs Cup final, this time against Juventus. For the first leg, in Italy, Don had us based in a mountain retreat, having allowed us to take along our wives, who would stay in town. But things did not work out quite as planned. It rained incessantly on the day of the match, and after 64 minutes, with us leading by a goal, their captain informed the referee that they could not possibly carry on playing in such conditions. He simply picked up the ball and marched his team off! The rules were such that no refund needed to be made to paying customers if the match had progressed for an hour. So they're losing 1–0, it's pissing down, they keep the gate money and the referee abandons the match!

What happened next was, I believe, the first hint that Don was beginning to lose his stranglehold on the club. The plan had been that we would join our wives in their hotel after the match on this Wednesday night and enjoy a party. But its abandonment meant that we were to play again on the Friday and Don announced that it was to be all-change. We were told that there would be no meeting up with our partners and that we were to go straight back to the mountains. He cannot have expected the response. Several players, no doubt under varying degrees of spouse pressure, protested vehemently and Don could not believe that one of his orders was being questioned. I could see in his mannerisms over the next few weeks that he had begun to feel that he was losing the players a little bit. Not completely. But it was there, that little seed of doubt. You could see where this was coming from. Some of the lads were mightily fed up of spending so much time in hotels away from their wives and children and for the first time, in Turin, a few frustrations boiled over. This was allied to a growing scepticism over Don's team talks, which could go on for hours and were filled with the most minute details of opponents' strengths and weaknesses. Maybe we should have listened a little bit more intently to his overviews sometimes, particularly the one at Colchester, but they really did test your powers of concentration.

How seriously could you take a dossier the thickness of a Ministry of Defence file on a team you knew to be inferior? At the end, our minds numbed, the lads would say: 'Is it Real Madrid we're playing, or Colchester?' What was filtering into our minds was that Don did not really believe in us. Don took these implied questions about his authority very personally. The Fairs Cup saga ended happily, however. Having drawn 2–2 in the replayed first leg with goals, unusually, from Paul Madeley and Mick Bates, we drew 1–1 at Elland Road, Clarke scoring, to win the trophy on the away goals rule.

chapter seven

BRIBERY AND CORRUPTION

HAVING WON OUR SPURS ON THE CONTINENT, MORE DOMESTIC SILVERWARE became the priority as we went into season 1971–72. As a squad, we were becoming that little bit older and it needed no pointing out to us that if we were to achieve the ultimate dream of winning the European Cup then first we had to win the league championship. In prioritising this it was accepted that the UEFA Cup, which replaced the Inter Cities Fairs Cup, should take a low priority and accordingly we were knocked out in the very first round by the Belgian side Liege. Having won the first leg at Elland Road 2–0 Don decided to field mostly youngsters in the return and we lost 4–0.

Our other minor brush with Europe that season featured a commemorative match between the first and last winners of the Inter Cities Fairs Cup, Barcelona and ourselves, and this resulted in a 2–1 win for the Spaniards.

Don was seemingly aware now of the over-commitment which had stifled our potential in previous seasons and our campaign was more structured. We enjoyed an excellent season which saw us win the FA Cup in its centenary year and figure in the closest finish imaginable to a league championship. We had previously suffered some indignities in the FA Cup, but this time all went according to plan.

Having thrashed Bristol Rovers 4–1 in the third round we had two games against Liverpool in the fourth round, beat Cardiff in front of 50,000 at Ninian Park in the fifth and Tottenham in the sixth, and we were served up a dream draw against Second Division Birmingham City at Hillsborough in the semi-final. We cantered it 3–0 for a Wembley date with Arsenal and were now very strongly fancied for the domestic double.

We duly beat Arsenal 1–0, through Clarke's lunging header from a Jones cross, but it was a final which is remembered for the dislocated elbow suffered by Mick Jones in a last-minute collision with their goalkeeper Geoff Barnett. Mick wanted to go up to meet the Queen and receive his medal – a dream he had always held – but the club doctor was very afraid that he would pass out with the pain and recommended that he miss out on the traditional ceremony. But Mick was not going to miss out on his moment of glory and after we had all received our medals Norman Hunter helped him all the way up the steps, where the Queen waited. Having come back down again Mick was taken straight off to hospital.

Crazily, our final league game of the season, away at Wolverhampton Wanderers, was scheduled for the Monday, 48 hours after the Cup final, but it came as a surprise to nobody that Don's pleas to the FA to put the game back fell on deaf ears. Relations between Don and Hardaker had been further soured by our manager's latest attempts to win favour. These involved the insistence upon a personal hearing, whenever one of our players was sent off, based on television 'evidence'. To back up his claims, he would enlist the help of friends who worked in television cutting rooms in providing footage of the incident in question and then get some expert to cut out the vital bit of film. So, what the FA panel would see would be the beginning and the end of a tackle with a relevant second or two of tape mysteriously missing. He had got away with it once or twice, but the FA cottoned on when referees started saying: 'There was a bit more to it than that.'

To win the FA Cup is a major event for any city, which will roll out the red carpet and host a day of celebration for its successful team, but instead of taking an open-top bus ride parading the trophy through Leeds we were stuck in a Midlands hotel awaiting the Monday night match. The championship was still undecided, and on this evening there were still three teams (Derby, Liverpool and ourselves) who could win it. Derby had completed their league programme with a 1–0 defeat of Liverpool, taking them to the top with 58 points. But, convinced that they would be overtaken by either Leeds or Liverpool, who also played on the Monday night against Arsenal, Derby had gone off on holiday to Majorca. We both lost – and Brian Clough's men were champions.

Had Don shown more belief in his squad he would have changed some of the personnel at Wolves. Jones was definitely ruled out anyway but Gray, heavily strapped, and Clarke, dosed up with pain-killing injections, were thrown into the fray. All of the players were tired from their Wembley exertions at the end of a long, hard season, but three or four of them were a maximum 70 per cent fit. And it was not only the physical side of things which counted against us. Mentally, the build-up to the Cup final was massive and exhausting. It was the 100th final, the Queen was going to be there and the media interest was intense.

We won it, but there was no celebration. There was a banquet in the team hotel, but only the wives could go to it. We were put on a bus and off we went straight from Wembley up the motorway to Wolverhampton without even a glass of champagne. We had had nothing to eat or drink at Wembley and we stopped at the first motorway services out of London for a cup of tea and a grotty sandwich. 'Great winning the Cup, isn't it,' one of the lads said, and it just about summed up the situation. But Don was nothing if not a pro. We had the game, a massive game, to play on the Monday and that was the sole agenda now.

In the build-up to the game at Molineux the jungle drums were beating. A draw was all we needed from the game to clinch the title and it was heavily rumoured that somebody from the Leeds camp had tried to get at the referee. This allegation was fuelled by an article written by Gary Sprake, who had now departed the club, in which it was suggested that Revie, with some involvement from Bremner, had tried through contacts to offer inducements to the Wolves players to take it easy. Indeed, two of their players confirmed that they had been approached. This was heavy stuff, which was set to go to court. Sprake had the knives out. He had been dropped for our FA Cup semi-final against Birmingham in favour of David Harvey, missed out on an FA Cup winner's medal and left the club to join, coincidentally, Birmingham.

Revie and Bremner won the case, with Billy receiving £100,000, the biggest out-of-court settlement in the game's history, and Don deciding not to pursue the matter. The facts of what really happened are a matter of conjecture, but what is indisputable is that many, too many, suspect things happened in the game itself, and particularly involving Leeds in both advantageous and disadvantageous circumstances, for there to be certain knowledge that football was whiter than white.

That is the way the game was during this period in its history. There was very little money in football for players, managers or referees. The officials, who operated on a pretty amateurish basis, in particular must have been very vulnerable to people approaching them with offers. I don't know what kind of money would be considered to be sufficient inducement in those days, but with players on, say, £150 a week and referees on perhaps £10 a match, an offer of £1,000 would have been sufficient to force an examination of conscience and morals. And for players, this would not necessarily mean chucking it; more a case of not giving full commitment. I am making no accusations because I have no incontrovertible proof, but I remain utterly convinced that football in general was awash with illegal incentive money. Bribery, if you like. I was never approached personally, but then I was part of a team which was always going for championships and trophies. It would have been more opportunistic to target teams which were second, third and fourth bottom of the league who, with one or two games to go, were in danger of neither winning anything nor being relegated; teams for whom results had no significance. To finish the season with a grand, or £10,000 between them, would pay for a family holiday and damn near buy a house in those days. I can well imagine these players thinking: 'I'm going on holiday tomorrow and the last thing I want is to be involved in a kicking match with Leeds. No broken arms. No broken legs. I just want to get this game out of the way and go.'

At Wolves, in front of 53,000, the game was only a few minutes old when, from our throw-in, their full-back, Bernard Shaw, actually had the ball in his hand in his own penalty area for what seemed like five seconds frozen in time. It just had to be a penalty. Bernard dropped the ball in the acceptance that he had given away a spot kick but, wholly mysteriously and blatantly wrongly, it was not given. But so rife had been the rumours about this game being bent that I would imagine the referee was absolutely petrified about the prospect of having to officiate in the game in the first place, let alone award a penalty. Wolves, who were ninth in the league, had absolutely nothing to play for – but they played like a team who had been given £100,000 a man to win. All the speculation had put them in a funny position. The prospect, if they had been beaten 3–0, was that the headlines would suggest they had taken a dive. Far from that scenario, they went at us tooth and nail and took a 2–0 lead through Munro and Dougan. They played brilliantly, steaming into tackles, and their goalkeeper Phil Parkes had the game of his life. Though Bremner pulled one back, they survived a late onslaught to leave us runners-up in the league for the fifth time in eight seasons. One of the accusations after the match was that, with five minutes to go, Bremner had offered one of their players a serious sum of money to hack him down in the penalty area.

Having lost, we were convinced that Liverpool, with only one defeat in their previous 16 games and fresh as daisies, would have cashed in at Arsenal. But they did not. A goalless draw was not good enough, and to rub salt into their wounds two minutes from time, with their fans chanting 'Leeds are losing', they had a goal by John Toshack disallowed for a marginal offside. That left Derby, with such performers as McFarland, Todd, Gemmill, Hector, O'Hare and Hinton, to uncork the bubbly in their Spanish resort. The joy felt by their Revie-hating manager Clough must have been unconfined. His feeling must have been that not only had he won the league, but in the process he had prevented Leeds from doing so.

Nevertheless, we had our open-top bus ride through the city, albeit in an atmosphere far removed from that associated with such events. It was as though we had lost the FA Cup final and this was some kind of wake. The expectation had been that we would win the double and the occasion was tinged with sadness because we had not done so. I always feel sad about that. Had we been going for the FA Cup alone, and had managed to win it, there would have been a carnival atmosphere, I am sure. We drove back to the Queen's Hotel, where Don had set up a champagne buffet, and none of the lads felt like it. It had been 48 hours since we won the Cup, we'd missed out on the championship and all we wanted to do was to go to a nightclub and get pissed together. With all due respect, we didn't want to sit in a formal atmosphere with the manager, the coaching staff and directors present. We wanted to get out among the people.

That season saw us welcome on board two very promising young Scottish players in Joe Jordan, from Morton, and Gordon McQueen, from St Mirren. We called Joe 'The Teuchter', Scottish slang for a Highlander. In his big woolly jumpers he really was playing the part of somebody who had come down from Scotland to the big city. Gordon was a big jovial lad who, on inspecting the club rule book for the first time, said: 'What's this? You're not allowed a drink after Thursday? Friday was our big night out just before a match at St Mirren.' Joe had been recommended by Bobby Collins and Gordon by John Barr, our scout in Scotland. Jack Charlton had reached the stage where his playing days were nearly at an end and Mick Jones was beginning to suffer terribly with his knees, so Joe and Gordon were being groomed as their successors. Of course, they both went on to enjoy fabulously successful careers, but just then at Leeds it was like the Scottish mafia with Bremner, Gray, Harvey, myself, Joe and Gordon in the squad.

All summer the stories rumbled on about Leeds: Sprake's accusations, the court case, the Wolves game. We were headlines every weekend. And whatever the facts, people make up their own minds. Since Sprake left the club he has never, so far as I can make out, been welcomed back, even when we held a 25th anniversary dinner to celebrate our FA Cup final win. I was asked by the Leeds commercial manager about my views on Gary being invited and my reply was that bygones should be bygones and that he should come. I was in a decided minority. Having phoned round the other players, he concluded that it might not be a good idea. For all his mistakes, he spent 11 years at Elland Road, making 507 appearances, having played his first game as an emergency reserve at Southampton as a 16-year-old. He was eventually replaced by David Harvey and joined Birmingham in 1973, retiring with a back injury two years later.

chapter eight

SHAME IN SALONIKA

A THUNDERSTORM ROLLED ROUND THE SALONIKA STADIUM IN GREECE AS WE came out for the 1973 Cup-Winners' Cup final against AC Milan, and these were appropriate conditions for what has gone down in Leeds' history as its most diabolical travesty. The majority of the 45,000 crowd was neutral and I wish that the same could have been said of the referee, a Greek named Christos Michas. I have already alluded to suspicious circumstances in the game as a whole, but suspicions were irrelevant in this particular game. It was wholly, indisputably and wretchedly bent. The tradition was to give a showpiece game such as a European final as a thank you to a local referee who was on the verge of retirement, and Michas was in that category. Before the game, John Giles who, along with Bremner, Clarke and Gray, was injured and had to miss the final, had picked up on stories that the Italians had taken steps to ensure that they would win the trophy come what may and he relayed to our team: 'There's no way we can win.' After just four minutes of the action we were given notice of the way the game would proceed when Michas mysteriously ruled that Paul Madeley had impeded one of their players, and from the free kick, 20 yards out, the ball deflected off our wall and past Harvey for what proved to be the only goal of the game. The only one that counted, that is. We played magnificently, producing 30 shots on goal and having numerous penalty appeals turned down, most notably when Jones was blatantly tripped in the box, when one of my crosses was deliberately handled by a defender and again when Jones was pushed.

The Greeks in the crowd started to voice their disapproval, chanting 'Shame . . . shame', as one decision after another went against us. The game blew up near the end when Hunter was chopped down as he tried to get away down the left. He retaliated and a mass brawl broke out near the touchline. Norman was sent off along with one of their players, but at the end the crowd left no one in any doubt about their feelings, jeering the Italians as they received the trophy and singing 'Ole, ole, Leeds, ole!' as we got our losers' medals. Again, when the referee went up for his medal, the chants of 'Shame . . . shame' went up. They were embarrassed by his shaming of their country. It was so obvious to the UEFA officials present that the game was crooked that Michas was banned for life the very next day. Milan were banned from European competition for four years. Nobody could prove that Milan Football Club had got at the referee. It might have been a Milan businessman, the mafia, anybody. But there was no question that somebody had.

One sad aspect of this was that I always thought that in horse racing, or any sport in which winners were deemed to have come by their victory illegally, the trophy would be taken off them and awarded to the rightful winner. When you ban a club for four years you must be hinting that they had some involvement in wrongdoing, otherwise what was the ban for? We were not given the trophy and I was always amazed that Leeds never took the matter any further. What had happened was just accepted.

The year 1973 is also memorable for one of the biggest upsets in FA Cup final history, our 1–0 defeat by Second Division Sunderland. In the semi-finals we had got our own back on Wolves for their depriving us of the league championship 12 months previously, beating them by the only goal of the game at Manchester City's Maine Road, scored by Billy Bremner. There was an element of luck in our victory because Wolves, who were in their pomp at this time, were the better side on the day. In the dressing-room afterwards we heard that Sunderland had beaten Arsenal in the other semi-final, and there was no containing the belief that the FA Cup had been put on a plate for us. The feeling was that the hard work had been done on our behalf, but at Wembley it didn't go according to the script.

Before the match, Sunderland were given no chance. No Second Division side had won the trophy for 42 years and over the 90 minutes we should have beaten them. There was a shock for everybody when Ian Porterfield scored from their first corner after 32 minutes, but we recovered our composure and began to grind away at them. On 65 minutes came the incident which I am still asked about by everybody. Paul Reaney put in the perfect cross for Trevor Cherry to head goalwards and it looked all over the equaliser, until their goalkeeper, Jim Montgomery, twisted in mid-air and palmed the ball away. I was lurking six yards out with the goal at my mercy and so certain was the BBC commentator David Coleman that I would score that he said: 'Lorimer . . . one–one.' Monty, and the fates, had other ideas. I had so much time that I had the luxury of thinking to myself: 'Right. Don't blast it. It might go over. Just nice firm contact back into the empty net and we're out of trouble.' I hit it just as I wanted to hit it, sweetly, right off the middle of my foot. Monty was on the ground and I turned with my arm in the air. But with a desperate effort the keeper raised himself and somehow the ball hit his elbow, cannoned onto the underside of the bar, bounced on the line and was scrambled to safety.

It was lovely for the next ten years, getting offers from Sunderland fans of a season ticket in case I should ever want to visit. But it was a place I didn't really want to go to! After games, when you've done something stupid or been guilty of an incredible miss, you worry about it. But that particular incident never concerned me. I had done exactly as I had wanted to do and it was a one-in-a-million save, which the goalkeeper knew nothing about, which prevented a goal. If I'd mishit it, it would have gone in. I would do exactly the same again. When I got back to the hotel my wife said: 'You look grey.' It was a bit of an embarrassment to me but, at the end of the day, there was nothing else I could have done.

I was to play 63 matches in that season (1972–73), having played 56 the previous season and 53 in the one before that. I was fairly lucky with injuries, and played 701 games in total for Leeds. That cup final double-header of a season began strangely. We were away to Chelsea on the opening day and I went in goal when David Harvey had to go off with concussion. We were reduced to nine men when Mick Jones limped out of the action and, unsurprisingly, we lost 4–0. I did goalkeeper training on a regular basis and must have been between the sticks for Leeds on half a dozen occasions. For our regulars it would be a surprising season in which Sprake, with his volatile temper, didn't punch somebody and get sent off, so we had to have an option.

Mick Bates had just come into the squad and, with injuries to both Bremner and Giles, he got quite a bit of match time in a season in which, unfortunately, the team began to break up. Jack Charlton had played just 18 games when he left to become the manager of Middlesbrough. It was very sad to see him go. He had been at Leeds since he was a boy and had become part of the furniture, despite unpromising beginnings in which he was seen by the older players at the club as a rebel without a cause. Big, raw and undisciplined, few rated him as a player until Don took him in hand. Jack was great to have around the place. He was just so funny, in the way that you would laugh at him rather than with him. For instance, our goalkeepers. Every single time we conceded a goal, no matter whether it was the keeper's fault or not, Jack would shout and scream abuse at him. And it didn't matter who he was. Even when West Germany scored in the 1966 World Cup final, the great Gordon Banks could not escape his wrath.

He was awful to play with. Many was the time that the explosive Jack and the volatile Gary Sprake had to be pulled apart in the dressing-room after matches. There were always major ructions. It wasn't so much a case of Gary being at fault or not, or the whole crowd pointing the finger of blame at the keeper, but Jack's inevitable reaction to a goal being conceded. I could understand Sprakey sometimes getting the needle with Jack, who always blamed the keeper. It was probably his clever way of diverting unwanted attention away from himself in many instances. Jack was a miserable sod in the dressing-room. At the start of the day all the lads would say 'Morning, Jack', and he would just grunt. He would throw his clothes onto his peg, pull on his shorts and his top and grab one of the papers which lay on a table in the middle of the room. Then he would be off to the toilet. Not a word. Every day the same. It became a joke.

One snowy, icy, deathly cold January day, when we had all tired of his attitude, we determined upon revenge. No matter that it was Jack Charlton, we were going to get him in a way he would never forget. The toilet being occupied by him was an open-top cubicle and always outside this was a basket-weave skip. Allan Clarke and John Giles had briefed the dressing-room boy to place in the skip two buckets of freezing-cold water in advance of Jack's arrival, and they waited until he had become comfortably positioned with his newspaper before letting their target have the contents simultaneously over his head. They legged it back to the dressing-room, and when Jack came in he eyed us all accusingly, though he had an idea that Giles, the practical joker of the camp, might be involved somewhere down the line. 'I suppose it was you, you little Irish bastard,' he said to Gilesey. 'No, not me, Jack,' he said. 'Leave me out of this one.' He looked at Clarkey and charged: 'I suppose it was you, you long skinny streak.' Sniffer, in his unmistakable Brummy accent, replied: 'Not me, Jack. You've got the wrong fellow.' It was quite obvious to Jack that none of us was going to be man enough to admit to the prank and he boomed: 'None of you, and I mean none of you, will ever have a shit in peace again while I am at this club.' He had a final put-down. As he stood there, with his long chin, and his long neck and the few strands of hair on his head down over his forehead, and dripping from head to toe, he said: 'I wouldn't care. It fucking missed.' You couldn't get one over on Jack.

He had a reputation for being tight. For instance, he would never buy cigarettes, and when he went along with Billy Bremner to 10

Downing Street following the award of their CBEs there were complimentary cigs in silver holders and he couldn't leave without putting three in his top pocket. On trains he would go up to perfect strangers and say: 'Give us a cig, mate.'

But he was an immense character. He was the type of man who would always rise to a challenge and we always said that he was a great centre-half when the centre-forward had rattled him in the first five minutes of a game with an elbow or studs in his leg. It would waken him up. He was very casual, but if somebody upset him that was it. All hell broke loose. I do not agree with those who feel he was overrated. I think he was a colossus as a centre-half. He won things with us and with England and I think he has a lot of reasons to be grateful to Don. Jack was certainly a man and a player to have around when the chips were down. Yet as much as he was a big, strong, domineering man who would throw the playing cards out of the team coach window because he could never win – and everybody was frightened of him to a degree – he was always the butt of the jokes because he was so easy to wind up.

The leaving of a football club is always strange, chiefly because it is usually unannounced. There will be a manager-to-player dialogue concerning an offer received by the club and you will turn up for training the next morning to find that your colleague, somebody who has served the club for many years and with whom you have worked day in and day out for an eternity, is no longer there. One day, Jack had gone to Middlesbrough. That was that. No more of the man we would refer to as 'The Big Pillock' without ever meaning it. He's actually got a heart of gold, and when you see and hear him on television panels nowadays he exudes warmth and sincerity. Of course he did very well in management, with Middlesbrough, Sheffield Wednesday and, in particular, the Republic of Ireland, where he is a folk hero. Once on the international scene he changed the style of play to one which I would never have enjoyed – direct, with the elimination of the midfield – but he and John Giles were the only two of the ex-Leeds players who went on to succeed as managers.

Three parties benefited from Jack's departure from Leeds. Our goalkeeper, who would now get some peace, rival goalkeepers, who would no longer have the impediment of a towering figure right on their goal-line from corners, ready to snaffle a Gray or Lorimer corner, and Christos Michas, whom he would surely have strangled.

chapter nine

REVIE: THE END

WE HAD FINISHED THIRD IN THE LEAGUE IN 1972–73, WHILE THE CHAMPIONS, for the first time in seven years, were Liverpool. The red half of Merseyside had always boasted a good side and over the years we enjoyed some tremendous battles with them. Now, in 1973–74, we were to win the championship, but the resurgent Liverpool went on to dominate English football for two decades. The great thing about Leeds and Liverpool, which still holds good today, is that the rivalry between managers, players and fans alike, is friendly. I have always admired the way in which Liverpool Football Club has conducted itself. Their policy of recruiting from within the club has been abandoned in recent times, but there was much to admire in the continuity brought by such appointments as Ronnie Moran, Bill Shankly, Bob Paisley, Joe Fagan, Kenny Dalglish and Graeme Souness.

That was where Leeds went wrong – in not appointing John Giles as successor to Don Revie. The choice of manager is critical to a club's well-being and the recent trend of bringing in foreigners has been a far cry from the soaraway success that some had imagined. The hapless Christian Gross at Tottenham is the outstanding example of overseas coaches whose reputations were bigger than their deliveries, in stark contrast to a host of excellent British managers, the doyen of whom, of course, is Sir Alex Ferguson. It's the old story. Somebody whispers in the ears of directors, 'You want a foreign coach', and their eyes light up. It's not working, and an entire rethink has been forced. You will never get away from the fact that Britain is different from the rest of the world. We're a different breed.

The summer of 1973 was an interesting time at Leeds. The humiliation of the FA Cup defeat, our indignation over events in Greece, the resentment which had built towards the club and a final league position of only third all served to fire us up for the forthcoming campaign and we started with all guns blazing. Such was our resolve and determination to square up matters that we won our first seven games, scoring 19 goals in the process, and went an amazing first 29 matches, from 25 August to 23 February, without defeat. That takes some doing. The sequence came to an end at Stoke where, with ten minutes to go, we led 2–0. But we mentally switched off, took our feet off the pedals, and they banged in three, with our ex-player Jimmy Greenhoff conjuring the last-minute winner. We were to lose further matches against Liverpool, West Ham and Burnley, but we cruised the league by five points from Liverpool.

This was despite the steady worsening of Mick Jones's knees, for which the Leeds medical staff of the time and Don Revie must, in my view, take their share of blame. What Mick was suffering was an early form of arthritis. He couldn't train, yet they persisted in firing cortisone injections into him to keep him on the field of play. Although Joe Jordan was coming on – he scored seven goals – he wasn't quite ready for the limelight and Mick battled on. He was terrific for us. Mick, Clarkey and myself shared no fewer than 65 goals between us, but there was no way Mick should have been playing towards the end. With rest and time between his matches his career could have been prolonged, and that he was asked to play game after game demonstrated a too-hard aspect of wanting to be successful. Mick was a wonderful, wonderful player with the heart of a lion. He would chase any lost cause. He never scored as many goals

ABOVE: I sign for Leeds United as a 15 year old in 1962
watched by my mum and dad, and Don Revie.

BELOW: One of my two goals for Scotland Schoolboys in a 4–1 defeat of England.

ABOVE: Celebrations in the Elland Road dressing-room after beating Juventus in the 1971 Fairs Cup final on the away goals rule.

BELOW: I'm medal-watching as Billy Bremner holds the FA Cup following our defeat of Arsenal in the centenary final at Wembley in 1972.

ABOVE: Billy Bremner is controversially ruled offside as I thunder home a shot in the 1975 European Cup final against Bayern Munich in Paris. We were luckless in a game which we went on to lose 2–0.

BELOW: Offside? You must be joking, ref. We protest after our controversial defeat by Bayern Munich in the 1975 European Cup final.

RIGHT: No Ferraris in those days – just my trusty Austin 1100.

BELOW: Pride and honour. One of my Scottish international caps.

ABOVE: Chips with everything. I'm at a sportsmen's evening organised by celebrated Yorkshire eatery Harry Ramsden's with Leeds United's John Charles (centre) and Eddie Gray.

BELOW: A day at the races, with Manchester United and England legend Nobby Stiles.

ABOVE: Bye bye Leeds. I salute the fans in the Kop after my
1977 testimonial against a Scotland XI.

BELOW: Hello Leeds. I rejoin the club from Vancouver in 1983 under Eddie Gray.

ABOVE: Lash . . . Rocket . . . Ninety. There was a stream of nicknames after I won a competition to discover the hottest shot in football. Of course 'Ninety' was an exaggeration, but at 76.8 m.p.h I won the trophy from the likes of Bobby Charlton, David Herd and Francis Lee.

BELOW: Teeing up for some relaxation away from football (left to right): myself, Les Cocker, Don Revie, Eddie Gray, Norman Hunter, Mick Bates, Terry Cooper, Mick Jones, Gary Sprake.

ABOVE: Behind the bar at my pub The Commercial in Leeds.

BELOW: Leaving Leeds for the last time in 1985.

as Clarkey and myself, but the number of goals he made for us, by his hard work and going up among the big lads, getting clattered and the ball falling for us, was almost incalculable. Mick had to work for his goals. We got the glory, yes, but without Mick we would never have got the ball, never mind the goals. He was an unsung hero, appreciated by the players but not always fully, I felt, by the fans.

We were all hopeful that after a summer's rest Mick would come back, but the damage that had been done by constantly playing someone who was less than 100 per cent fit and in pain was irreversible. He limped on a while, but he was forced to retire from the game in 1975 having scored 111 goals in 313 appearances. He went back to his birthplace, Worksop, opened a little sports shop and remains a nice, honest, quiet guy. Football is not all champagne and roses and I always think of Mick as the living proof of that.

Mick was a further departure from the team and it wasn't long before Terry Cooper joined Jack Charlton at Middlesbrough. Terry, who had seen Trevor Cherry holding down a regular place, was a smashing guy: a local lad from Ferrybridge, with a broad Yorkshire accent, and the son of a miner. Although he was a fabulous player, Terry was, I'm sure he would agree, a failed winger. He had been playing on the wing for the reserves, and although he was a fine player he didn't really have the necessary pace to fly down the line. What he did have was a great heart. Don had seen this and, much as he had done with another failed winger on the right in Paul Reaney, moved him to left-back. Leeds' 1992 championship-winning manager Howard Wilkinson claimed credit for introducing to the English game these things called wing-backs, which I find quite amusing. Some 20 years earlier Reaney and Cooper were referred to as overlapping full-backs and these beings, to my mind, were performing exactly the same roles. Yet the Wilkinson phraseology was received like some blinding new science. Don taught Reaney and Cooper how to defend and then, with their ability to get forward, we were able through Eddie Gray on the left and myself on the right to exert permanent pressure on both flanks.

Terry, a real crowd-pleaser with his tenacious tackling and his runs up the line, enjoyed a great career. Unfortunately, four games before our FA Cup final against Arsenal, he broke a leg and the injury was to keep him out for a full season. Coincidentally, the same thing happened to Reaney before the Sunderland final. Terry's break, of the left shin in a game at Stoke in April 1972, was a particularly bad one. The lads used to feel so sorry for him, but he showed tremendous courage to battle through it. His body was not producing calcium, and as the injury was not healing as it should have done he had to go on a Guinness and milk diet. He finished up around 15 stone. As the leg got better, his next problem was to get rid of the four stone of excess weight he had put on. When he left Leeds for Middlesbrough he had made 350 appearances and went on to play for Bristol City, Bristol Rovers and Doncaster, chalking up another 250 games. He endured an amazing personal battle to come back, when I am sure it would have been very easy for him to hold his hands up and say: 'That's enough.'

One person did take that course and that, almost unthinkably, was Don Revie. A lot of people said that the reason he left was that he did not want to be the one responsible for breaking up the team, and indeed it is the view of one of his successors, Jimmy Armfield, that it was he who had been saddled with the task of doing the dirty work. While accepting Don's sentiment – he thought a lot of all of us, and we of him – I cannot get away from an incident during that fabulous unbeaten run of ours. The 17th of these 29 matches saw us play out a goalless draw at Derby County and none of us could believe it when we were summoned to a right bollocking which finished with him lashing out: 'If you lot are not going to do it for me, then I'll bring in people who will.' Hell-bent on winning the league at all costs this season, and still smarting from the events of the previous season, I think he was at the end of his tether.

Now, nobody likes defeat. No professional wants to be beaten. Even if I am playing tiddlywinks with a four-year-old child, it is in me to thrash him. I could not let my kids beat me at anything, even to make them happy. So for Don to issue such a threat at a time when we were playing so fabulously was quite outrageous. We knew we had an ambitious manager. Now we had a ruthless one. From that moment on the players had a different feeling towards Revie. And he knew it. Whether he knew at the time that he was going to finish at the end of the season, that he was going out with the title come what may, and this was an attempt to bash us to the championship with a big stick, I don't know. These things were never done in the dressing-room after games. He always reasoned that the hour after a match was the wrong time for inquests, and that they were best left until everybody had had the weekend to think about what they had done wrong, what they might have done better and how things might be improved. In the heat of the moment people might say things they didn't really mean. He would let you know if he wasn't pleased, saying 'That was fucking awful' before storming out. And even then this fanatically superstitious man, who wore the same mohair suit with his arse hanging out of the trousers because he thought it was a lucky suit, took the very same route to the ground every day, walking twice round the same lamp-post, would go through the same routine, putting on his overcoat and combing his hair in front of the dressing-room mirror before making a hurried exit.

That particular meeting showed an ugly side of Don that had never before been evident. There were always frank exchanges at these post-training meetings on Mondays, but until then it was always constructive. His tirade changed everything. As far as the players were concerned, he had burned his bridges. There would always be the respect; we owed him a lot. But atmospheres change. You play for yourself and your team-mates, and you play for your manager if you respect him. Soured by the way Don had conducted himself, for the rest of the season we played for ourselves.

The campaign had its usual talking points. Don had decided that we were to have no interest in the two domestic cups and the UEFA Cup, and after we had drawn at Bristol City, seventh from the bottom of the Second Division, in the fifth round of the FA Cup, we replayed on the Wednesday afternoon because of the power cuts which were affecting the country at the time. Bristol's young Scottish striker Don Gillies scored midway through the first half what proved to be the only goal of the game and they went on to a quarter-final meeting with Liverpool. We had gone out of the League Cup to Ipswich at the first hurdle and this left the European scene, in which we actually bet a substantial amount of money against ourselves. Having beaten the Norwegian side Stromsgodset in the first round, Don said: 'We want out of this. It can only hinder us in the league.' Our second round opponents were Hibernian, and the first leg at Elland Road finished goalless. A fortnight later, in the return, Don left out the great majority of the experienced players and replaced them with young Scottish lads like goalkeeper John Shaw. He included Billy Bremner and myself because we were Scots and might enjoy going north of the border and inviting our families along. His instruction was that we were not to be busy and should just cruise through the game.

My local bookmaker, Peter Fairbairn, like every other bookie, naturally had us long odds-on to win, while Hibs were chalked up at 3–1. I told him it was impossible for us to win with all the kids and asked if he could get a big bet on our Scottish hosts. The lads pooled together £500, a lot of money then, Peter doubled it and got the bet on. Billy was playing sweeper – that's how seriously Don was taking it – and he was back-heeling it here, messing about there and joking his way through the game. Unfortunately, young John in goal was wanting to make a name for himself. He was not in on the scam and was flinging himself left and right, making fabulous saves, until he got injured and had to go off. He was replaced by an even younger lad, a Welsh kid called Glan Letheran, and we thought: 'We're in here. Glan will be nervous.' Sure enough, he was just as agile as John had been and, come what may, Hibs could not get the ball in the net until, with ten minutes to go, they broke clear down the right, the cross came over and their inside-forward headed home. We gave each other a knowing look, winked and whispered: 'Thank God for that.' But the linesman had only put his flag up for offside, and despite our protestations that it was all right the goal was disallowed.

At full time, with the scores level, we had done our money. All bets are settled, of course, on 90 minutes. It went to penalties and Don's view was that, having come so far, we might as well do our best now to win it. Damned right! We needed to win the match to collect our bonuses to cover the bet! And win it we did. The next round pitted us against the Portuguese team Setubal and how seriously we took this can be gauged from the fact that we played golf on the afternoon of the game over there. We were duly knocked out.

Don Revie was confirmed as the successor to Sir Alf Ramsey as England manager on 4 July 1974. After his appointment he said: 'I made the first move. They did not contact me. I fancied being England manager.' Don had excellent qualifications for the job. He had been a talented inside forward, winning six England caps while with Manchester City, and had transformed Leeds from a struggling Division Two outfit to being the most feared side in the land. He was not, however, a universal first choice. London-based journalists hated him. If anything bad was written about Leeds he would ban the author of the article from the stadium. No messing. He would ring up the editor and tell him not to bother sending the journalist to the next match because he would not be allowed in. And he meant it. He was a bit like a mafia boss – you don't talk about my team, you don't talk about me, or you're out whether you're right or wrong. You just don't say it. The northern journalists were fine. They understood Don and he treated them very well. He would give them anything they wanted. They were allowed to travel with the team on the coaches, the trains, and the aeroplanes and they had full access to the players. Fleet Street was a different matter, and that may have been because Leeds always beat the teams from the capital. The north was cleaning up in football through ourselves, Liverpool and Manchester United, while London teams like Tottenham, Chelsea and Arsenal were having a nightmare.

Getting the England job gave Don the rationalisation that in leaving

Leeds he was in no way being traitorous. And, in fact, he left Leeds in a very healthy state. We were the reigning champions, there was £2 million in the bank and there were some smashing young players, Jordan, McQueen, Terry Yorath, Frank Gray and the like, coming through. He lasted three years in the job, with an acceptable record of 14 wins in 29 internationals, before going to the United Arab Emirates for a tax-free £60,000 a year plus bonuses. The general consensus was that he had discovered a yawning chasm between the day-to-day running of a league club and the management of the national team. Don's club success was built on the nurturing of a tremendous loyalty between himself and the players. That is evident in none of us leaving over a period of many years, despite the pile of offers on his desk. At international level things would be very different. There would be only the odd getting-together of a diverse collection of players, some of whom Don would have difficulty in tolerating.

Showboating players like Stan Bowles, Frank Worthington and Rodney Marsh, wonderful artists that they were, would certainly not have been his cup of tea. Nor would the 'Jack the Lad' types such as Alan Ball and Kevin Keegan, and the feeling would be reciprocal. The difficulty Don would have would be in imparting his family unit values, working and living for each other, to such players. And the faction that wanted to see such flashy football, without necessarily winning, got their way. Don's *bête noire*, Alan Hardaker, said: 'Don Revie's decision does not surprise me in the slightest. Now I only hope he can quickly learn how to call out bingo numbers in Arabic.' This was a reference to one of Don's chosen forms of pre-match entertainment for the players, and there was no less vitriol in the reaction of the FA secretary Ted Croker, who said: 'The committee unanimously deplores the action of Don Revie. The FA is taking legal advice.' In fact the FA imposed a ten-year ban on Don, and though this was overturned in the High Court he did not escape without incurring the wrath of Mr Justice Cantley, who called his defection: 'A sensational, outrageous example of disloyalty, breach of duty, discourtesy and selfishness.'

chapter ten

OPPORTUNIST BREMNER

WHEN, IN THE SUMMER OF 1974, REVIE ACCEPTED THE ENGLAND JOB, HE SAW John Giles as the obvious choice as his successor and made that recommendation to the board. Highly respected by all the players, his knowledge of football was second to none and the Leeds chairman Manny Cussins was making absolutely the correct decision when he contacted John to say that he had been recommended and would, indeed, be the next manager of the club. John and I were golf partners – we were very close – and he called me with the glad tidings. Everything was in place for him to sign a contract the next morning.

But opposition was stirring in the background. Someone from the club's administrative staff contacted Billy Bremner to inform him of the impending appointment, and our captain's reaction was to contact the chairman to reveal his own ambition to become manager. When John arrived at the pre-arranged time of 9 a.m. the next day, Billy's car was already parked. Why, he wanted to know, was Giles getting the job ahead of him?

This eleventh-hour move by Billy came as little surprise to those of us who knew him. A truly fantastic colleague on the pitch – he would fight any battle and spill any amount of blood on behalf of his team-mates out there on the park – he was never quite the same man off it.

What mattered most in life to Billy Bremner was Billy Bremner and his welfare. He was totally self-centred. Don had kidded him a bit through the years about his potential to be a manager to get the best out of him. I don't think he really ever truly believed it. This was a ploy he used to keep Billy sweet.

The 9 a.m. meeting never happened. When it had got to 9.30, with the press waiting for the big announcement, Don asked the secretary, Keith Archer, to go and see the chairman to ask what was happening. John, he said, was raring to get started and needed to get into the dressing-room in his new capacity. The chairman agreed to see John and when he arrived he was told that the appointment would not be made there and then; more time was needed to think about it. Straightaway John, being the man of honour that he is, said that he had never asked for the job but had been recommended, and that if there was a problem then the chairman should count him out of it.

There is no doubt that it was the intervention of Billy which prevented John from getting the job. The chairman would be thinking: 'The captain wants the job. There might be trouble in the camp if he doesn't get it.' He maybe thought that Billy had a bigger influence on the players than was actually the case. Yes, Billy was an inspirational captain and a great footballer with a great attitude on the pitch. But I don't think anybody would have put him in the same category as Giles in club management terms. The respect of the players was paramount and Giles, who was very highly thought of by his team-mates, would have had that instantaneously.

That they failed to appoint Giles was to backfire heavily on the club. It was a decision which instigated the start of its decline. I am sure that if John had been given the reins, as Don had wished, Leeds United would have gone from success to success, given the healthy state in which Don had left it. That £2 million in the bank may even have been a conservative figure, given that these were the days in which the directors had a divi at the end of the season, leaving a 'pot' amount. They certainly hadn't paid the players fortunes and the scale of transfer fees can be gauged from Allan Clarke's British record fee of

£165,000 when he joined us. Within three years of a rise similar to ours, Celtic were skint, prompting searching inquiries in Scotland into where the money went. You look at our crowds of between 40,000 and 50,000 every match and realise that two matches would have paid the wages of the entire staff for a year. Add to the argument the fact that we bought hardly any players for years and it does make you wonder.

I have always said that if you had taken five drunks off the local Holbeck Moor at that time and given them that club, with that money, they could not have knackered the club more efficiently and more effectively than the directors proceeded to do. They achieved the impossible. They had all those fine young players coming through to blend with those of us who had all the experience, including a Giles who had now resigned himself to carry on playing, and it could not have been better teed up.

Brian Clough's hatred of Leeds was well documented. In numerous radio, television and newspaper interviews his criticism of the club was, at times, quite vicious, so it sent shockwaves through the game when he was installed at Elland Road as the man to take over the Revie baton. Let's be fair about Clough. His record as a manager speaks for itself. To win two European Cups with a small club like Nottingham Forest and their team of good professionals but only average players, and a league championship with almost as small a club in Derby County, takes some doing and bestows great credit on the man. But he was the wrong man for Leeds, as his laughably short tenure of 44 days demonstrates. He and his trusted right-hand man Peter Taylor had split at Forest, and the calming influence that Taylor had upon Clough, who was outspoken, controversial and often outrageous, was widely recognised in the game. Maybe Clough needed Taylor with him at Leeds, but his number two went south to manage Brighton instead.

Clough was on holiday when he was appointed and declared that he would not be interrupting his break to rush to Leeds. We reported back for pre-season training to be taken by Jimmy Gordon, a Scot who had worked alongside Clough at Derby. When the new boss arrived, he said nothing other than 'Good morning' to anybody for five days. On the Friday he called a meeting in the players' lounge and addressed us thus: 'You might be wondering why I haven't said a lot this week. The reason is that I have been forming my own opinions. That is what I like to do. I don't like listening to other people.'

This was acceptable enough, but what he went on to say greatly concerned us. 'Before we start working together with you lot I feel there are things that need to be said about each of you.' We knew it was coming then. He started from the goalkeeper and worked his way through the entire squad to left-wing. The comments were all derogatory, and when it came to my turn he repeated what he had told the audience at that sports awards dinner just a few years previously. Last on the list was Eddie Gray, one of the most popular guys in the team who had been terribly unlucky with injuries. 'As far as you're concerned, Gray,' said Clough, 'if you were a racehorse you would have been put down years ago.'

His concluding words were: 'I might as well tell you now. You may have won all the domestic honours and some European honours, but as far as I am concerned you can all throw every one of your medals in the bin. You never won any one of them fairly.' Don Revie did not escape lightly. Clough, having refused to sit in the office chair which had been occupied by his predecessor and ordered replacement furniture, was heavily critical of him. This was not terribly smart of Clough. Here were 16 internationals, close-knit, the best of pals and not untalented, being torn limb from limb. The effect was that we, as reigning champions, lost our first game of the 1974–75 season 3–0 to Stoke City and proceeded to take just four points from seven games. It was quite obvious that the board had made a big mistake. We had a midweek League Cup tie at Huddersfield on 10 September in which I scored a last-minute equaliser to force a replay, and on the coach on the way home the chairman told the manager that he would like him to go home with him to have a drink and a chat about things.

That was the last we saw of Clough. A week previously our vice-chairman Sam Bolton, who was also president of the FA, convened a meeting with the players at which we voiced our discontent. Sam had not agreed with Clough's appointment in the first place – it was a split board – and at this meeting he called Clough into the room. Straight to his face Sam, a tough-talking, bluff Yorkshireman, said: 'The lads do not think you are any good as a manager.' Just like that. He asked Clough for his response and, of course, the exchange was heated. The chairman was also in the room and Bolton said to Cussins: 'I told you we should never have appointed this man.' Not wishing to take responsibility, Cussins replied: 'I was not the only one.' The writing was on the wall. Clough reportedly received in the region of £250,000 and a brand new Mercedes, which was not bad work if you could get it. He had picked up in six weeks what we battled for 20 years to earn, so he didn't come out of it too badly.

Clough brought in three players with him from Nottingham Forest: John O'Hare, John McGovern and Duncan McKenzie. O'Hare did quite well for us and the fans took to him, but the same could not be said of McGovern. He had been Clough's captain at Forest, was a lovely lad and would run through a brick wall for you. But he wasn't a Leeds United-type player. He was out of his depth, even in training. The fans cottoned on to this and were merciless in their criticism.

I would never say that Clough was not a good manager. He was just the wrong appointment for Leeds, and the seeds were sown for the running-down of the club by the board. They brought in Jimmy Armfield, who was a very nice, knowledgeable man, but not strong enough to manage a big club like Leeds. The lads would always say: 'His indecision is final.' I think he was in awe of a situation in which the requirement was to be brave and strong and possess the ability to stand up and be counted. He had been a great player, an international of some repute, but his managerial experience was in the lower divisions at Bolton, where he had won the Division Three championship. It was unfair on Jimmy to have brought him in with an agenda of calming the troubled waters. He had been operating with young lads and done quite well with them, but now he was among seasoned pros. Again, Giles would have been the wise choice because he would have known what he was doing.

Within days of Armfield's appointment we were starting our European Cup campaign, so he had plenty on his plate. In fairness to him, he did well. Our poor start to the league campaign dictated that we would not qualify for Europe, but what we did do was to get to the 1975 European Cup final in what would be our last appearance in the flagship competition for many years. It was no easy passage to Paris. We beat Anderlecht in the quarter-finals and prevailed in a two-leg battle with the Cruyff and Neeskens-inspired Barcelona in the semis to book our place in the final against Bayern Munich. It was a nightmare of a match. We totally outplayed the Germans and it seemed we had taken a deserved lead after 66 minutes when Beckenbauer headed the ball out and I smashed home a volley from 16 yards right into the top corner. We were all convinced it was a goal, and I was utterly convinced, because I always looked at the referee before beginning my celebration and he was pointing to the centre circle. Then Beckenbauer took charge. He rushed across to the linesman and began to remonstrate with him, and this, in my view, panicked the official in a similar way to the Russian linesman in England's 1966 World Cup final. Was it a goal, was it not? Beckenbauer was known in the game for running referees and here he had already got away with a diabolical foul on Allan Clarke in the box. After consultations with his linesman the referee ruled that Billy Bremner had been in an offside position when my shot went in and disallowed the goal.

We were crestfallen. The minds of all of us went back to the robbery in Greece two years previously. Here we were again, victims of a diabolical decision on a big occasion, and the fans, certainly, had had enough. Unfortunately they erupted violently, and the rioting became steadily worse when Bayern scored from a breakaway within six minutes of our ruled-out goal. Nine minutes from time the Germans sealed it with a second goal, but by then our shape and discipline had gone. What was so sad was that 14 years on from the birth of the Revie dream of conquering Europe we were within touching distance only to have it snatched away. There was also the realisation that, a three-year European ban because of the behaviour of our fans notwithstanding, this would be our last crack at it because the time for the total disbanding of the squad was nigh.

We finished ninth in the league. Even the younger players at the club, like Jordan and McQueen, did not take to Jimmy, who was easy to wind up. One day in training we were all jogging along and McQueen, who was injured, was standing on the sidelines just playing keep-up with a ball. As we went past the young Scot we all started querying why he was being allowed to juggle with a ball when he was supposed to be injured. And as we passed on the next circuit Jimmy shouted: 'Gordon, stop keeping that ball up and get jogging round with the rest. Do as you're told.' With that, McQueen picked up all of 20 balls and kicked them one by one over the big fence separating the training ground from Jackson's Boilers. 'If I can't kick them,' he said, 'no fucker can kick them.' This underlined the lack of respect for the manager. Despite their antipathy towards him, Jimmy would not have a go back at Jordan and McQueen. He would always skirt round issues concerning them. I remember telling Jimmy that there were players at Elland Road, these two young Scots chief among them, who did not want to be there. Manchester United wanted both and they didn't want to play for us, yet he persevered with them.

One of the good things that Jimmy did was to introduce a close season tour of Marbella. Don had never done that. We went straight to the Spanish resort from the European Cup final amid rumours that John Giles was going to West Bromwich Albion in return for their player Len Cantello and a £100,000 adjustment in their favour. On the way down the lads goaded Armfield with: 'Hey, is that right? The papers have got it wrong. Shouldn't the money be the other way round? Fucking Len Cantello and Johnny Giles?' That's how the lads would speak to the manager. Although Jim had done well, everybody knew that this trip was the beginning of the end. He had this habit of sending players to other individuals with messages that he wished to see them before picking his team. You would go in and he'd say: 'How do you think you're playing?' You would reply: 'I'm not playing bad. I've not really been getting the service out on the wing,' and if you put a strong enough case he would hesitate and come back with: 'I'll tell you what. McKenzie's not playing very well, is he?' He wanted the lads to dob each other in and tell him who to pick. It got so bad that eventually, with a game against Liverpool coming up, Gilesey said to him: 'Look. If you want to drop me, fucking drop me. Don't be asking me about other players.'

All sorts went on on that little trip and the top and bottom of it was that Jimmy had totally lost the plot with the lads in a very short time. Giles was as miserable as sin, because he had had this offer from West Brom and just did not want to be at Leeds any more. I think he had been deeply traumatised by all the recent events at the club and, again, Jimmy got it wrong with him. Giles could have been a tremendous ally, but the manager wrongly pinned his faith in Billy Bremner who, to be quite honest, wasn't going to do him any favours. Billy just didn't rate him. He would have been better off keeping John and letting Billy go.

There is no question that John Giles was the best player I ever played with. Billy was the inspirational leader; John was the brains. When things were going wrong John would steady the ship. His passing ability, right and left, from 10 yards or 40 yards, was exemplary – he could drop them on a tanner – and he was also, I am sure he would tell you, one of the nastiest little bastards who ever pulled on a football jersey. There were a lot of so-called hardmen in the game at the time, but not a single one of them would ever take on Giles. He was only small, but how he could look after himself. One night we were playing a Turkish side in Ankara and they included in their team a little guy who was stereotypically built like a brick shithouse and whose job it was to mark John. You received no protection from referees in Europe in those days. You took what you got. This guy kicked John all over the park for 90 minutes and our player emerged with blood and mud all over his shorts because every time he had got the ball the Turk had steamed into him. At the end of the game Eddie Gray and I, our kit as white as when we kicked off because we had been out there on the flanks, were laughing. We thought it quite funny that John was cursing and swearing to himself, and looking so battle weary, but he saw no humour in this and as he looked at us he snarled.

When he looked the other way the little Turk was also laughing at him, and there and then professional suicide was committed. John, irately waving his finger in his opponent's face, said something to him along the lines of he would see him at Elland Road in a fortnight, and he laughed again. Two weeks later, the Turk was laughing on the other side of his face. In the dressing-room beforehand, John told Norman Hunter to roll his first pass of the game a couple of yards short. That, in football, is known as the suicide ball, and Norman, never the quickest on the uptake, protested. But out on the pitch Norman did as he had been asked and, sure enough, the Turk took the bait. John was like a matador. He stood to one side, leaving his foot in to fell the Ankara Assassin as he roared in. The snap of his leg could be heard all round the stadium and the stretcher-bearers raced into action. It was a mystery how the ambulance arrived on the scene so quickly, but the Elland Road telephonist swore that Giles had booked the ambulance for the Turk before he went out to play. John, of course, denies this. By the end of the game the casualty was back at the ground on crutches. He came into the players' lounge, where we were sitting with a drink, and sought sympathy for his injury. 'Fuck off,' said John.

Giles, who had joined Leeds from Manchester United directly after winning an FA Cup winner's medal in 1963, scoring 115 goals in 527 appearances, took up his managerial appointment at West Brom in 1975. In the space of two years he elevated them from the Second Division to a position where they would qualify for Europe. At Leeds, meanwhile, the lack of discipline was becoming almost total. Footballers need only an inch to take a mile, and in Jimmy Armfield we had a manager who could be manoeuvred. Unusually for Leeds, 1975–76 proved to be a season of little consequence. We were knocked out of the FA Cup in the fourth round by Crystal Palace, Notts County eliminated us in the early stages of the League Cup and a fifth-place finishing position in the league was the best we could muster.

When Tony Currie joined us from Sheffield United for £240,000 in the wake of the departure of both O'Hare and McGovern, it was a great acquisition. He was a smashing lad who really could have been a better player. He was a bit lazy on himself – one of those players who found great favour with the fans because of his skills but never really fulfilled his true potential. To my mind he should have been an England player for many years.

The exit of O'Hare and McGovern illustrated that the continuity which had been Leeds' trademark was no longer in evidence. We arrived at work to a new set of transfer rumours every day until it became a standing joke. Until now we had never had a time in an uneasy atmosphere or where there was unrest, but the tragedy here was that while it existed nobody really cared. To most experienced minds the managerial situation and the disappointment of not winning the European Cup made a decline inevitable and the attitude was: 'Well, if I'm the next one to go then fair enough.'

For a team that was used to challenging for everything this went totally against the grain, and early in the 1976–77 season both Billy Bremner and Norman Hunter left. Billy went off to play for Hull and Norman to Bristol City, while Jimmy brought in Ray Hankin from Burnley. There was movement in all directions and it is not difficult to imagine the atmosphere in the dressing-room. It was a sad time, and unsurprisingly we finished tenth in the league behind Liverpool, with the likes of Ipswich, Aston Villa and Newcastle above us. So, too, were West Brom, whom Gilesey had transformed.

It was very sad when Norman left the club. He was totally loyal to his team-mates; Leeds United through and through and a wonderful guy who would run through brick walls for you. All Norman wanted to do in life was to play football. Don had taken him from being a very ordinary inside-forward to one of the most respected players in the English game. I always felt that Norman was unlucky to be playing in the same position as the England captain, Bobby Moore. Norman provided much food for thought in Leeds that he should be in the international team ahead of his West Ham counterpart. My own view is that had they both been at Leeds then Norman would have been the first choice because of the way in which Leeds played. But England played differently, and Moore was the right man for his country, especially under the managership of Sir Alf Ramsey. Moore was a wonderful player who passed the ball beautifully and read the game well; a suave performer and a London smoothie, whereas Norman could play in no other way than with his normal, aggressive attitude. And you could not have played them both in the same side.

Norman was not a calculating player in the way that Giles was. He was just hard, though a little bit on the slow side, like other hardmen in the game such as Tommy Smith at Liverpool and Ron Harris at Chelsea. All these guys had a motto, which was 'All right, the ball will go past me, but you're not going with it.' Plain and simple. Norman was just the same in training. If you knocked one past him he wouldn't violently whack you across the knees, but you'd go up in the air all the same. He'd just smile at you and say: 'Sorry about that.' He wasn't sorry at all!

Norman was a lovely lad from Gateshead, up in the football-mad North-east. The fans, who affectionately christened him 'Bite Yer Legs', loved him. When he left, with 726 appearances under his belt, it was official confirmation that Leeds, as we knew them, had gone. He was followed out of the club by Terry Yorath, a man I always failed to get a handle on. I could never understand him. He was a very good, competitive player, but when he was given the No. 10 shirt that Giles had worn he, for some reason, started to think that he should attempt to play in the way that Giles had done. He was a terrific winner of the ball, a good passer and a driving force in the team, as he later showed when captaining Coventry, Tottenham and Wales, but he would not play his natural game. Much as I admired him, he did not have the awareness and the vision of Giles. He began to get caught in possession all the time and, unfortunately, the crowd first turned on him and then proceeded to give him a horrendous time.

When he had first come into the side he showed huge potential and was beginning to mature at such a rate that Armfield, intent on playing the extra midfield man, preferred him to Eddie Gray in our starting line-up for the 1975 European Cup final, which came as a surprise to many people. Most sportsmen are good at one thing. I wasn't a tackler, like a Hunter or a Giles, or a dribbler like a Gray. I was a direct player, reasoning that there was no need for me to beat a man when I could pass the ball 30 yards to take him out of the game. Why beat him first and then pass it? One of the elements of being a good footballer is knowing what your capabilities are. We would all like Giles's brain, Gray's graceful ball skills and Bobby Charlton's lovely, flowing movement, but at the end of the day you have only got what you have been given. One of the hardest things for a player is to know and accept his limitations. Terry, unfortunately, did not. He was hounded out. And he was a great loss to a club which was sinking fast.

An interesting postscript to the fledgling managerial careers of both Giles and Charlton was that each resigned his position, at West Brom and Middlesbrough respectively, within 24 hours of one another. 'We are on the crest of a slump,' said Jack, poetically, while John was more wounded. 'The job should come with a health warning,' he said. 'Football, and management, are precarious professions. There is so much fear in the game and it spreads like the plague.'

chapter eleven

BOSS'S INDECISION IS FINAL

JIMMY ARMFIELD TRIED. HE BROUGHT IN BRIAN FLYNN AND RAY HANKIN FROM Burnley, Arthur Graham from Aberdeen and Paul Hart from Blackpool, while Carl Harris was upgraded from the juniors. But he had lost his way, most importantly with the younger players who had by now realised his weaknesses. Even the most junior players were not paying the manager the respect that his position warranted, though this was understandable when the behaviour of Joe Jordan and Gordon McQueen was witnessed by them. Both played for Leeds only until halfway through the 1977–78 season and they would be the first to tell you that their minds were not on the job in hand. Pastures new beckoned for them and after one particular game against Newcastle, which we had lost 2–0 with only token efforts from the Scottish pair, Jimmy sounded off at the whole team.

I said: 'Never mind having a go at everybody. Talk to Joe and Gordon. They want to leave the club and the rest of the lads are trying their socks off.' Joe held up his hands and said: 'Sorry, lads. I let you down today. I'm here in body, but not in spirit.' Off he went to the old enemy, Manchester United, which was a hanging offence in Leeds, to be closely followed by his pal Gordon. I'm sure once Joe arrived at Old Trafford he would let it be known that big Gordon wasn't happy at Elland Road and would be available. When Gordon signed for Manchester United on 9 February 1978, the fee of £495,000 was a record deal between two English clubs. Joe went on to enjoy a great career in Italy and the loss to Leeds of players of their calibre was a mortal blow.

Their leaving was, I'm afraid, inevitable. Things had degenerated to the extent that during an FA Cup encounter with Manchester City at Elland Road, which we lost 2–1, Gordon openly engaged in fisticuffs with our goalkeeper, David Harvey. When that happens on the field it is indicative that the spirit in the dressing-room has completely gone. They were pals who played together for Scotland, and what we saw in Gordon was a young man whose frustrations had boiled over. This match was televised and the main talking point thereafter was that all could not be well behind the scenes at Leeds United who, because of the crowd trouble which further marred the game, were made to play the following season's cup ties away from home.

We paddled through a season which was notable only for its mediocrity in our finishing ninth in the league. Ray Hankin, a good, big lad, was top scorer with 20 goals but, again, Jimmy wasn't the ideal man to be handling such large-as-life characters. Ray needed strong handling. Along with Tony Currie he had a liking for the drink – we all liked a few drinks – and they would indulge more than the rest. Ray and Tony, fine players that they were, were not the best of trainers, with Ray in particular a heavy individual who needed driving. Off the field, Leeds United Football Club had become Leeds United Social Club. There was no ambition to win things. There would be a bit of training, but the main business of the day would be the extra-curricular arrangements and the social members would gather for an afternoon's drinking, often in Wetherby.

After one session in the town's wine bar we had gone on and left a worse-for-wear Hankin to fend for himself. I picked him up the next morning to learn that he had been pulled over by a copper. I said: 'Why didn't you get out of your car and run across the fields? You're a young lad.'

'Run?' he said. 'I couldn't even stand up!'

In court the arresting officer said that when he had asked Mr Hankin to get out of the car he 'seemed to have difficulty in keeping his balance'.

Although we were aware of these activities at other clubs they had never previously happened at Leeds. By this time I had got into the same mode. I was coming to the end of my career, I wasn't playing regularly – eight goals in 30 games, mostly in midfield, was my contribution – the atmosphere round the club had gone and I wasn't going to fall out with anybody. I just went along with the enjoyment. But it was not right, and I am not proud of it. The poor fans had witnessed the downturn in fortunes and a home fixture against Derby late that season attracted a crowd of just 16,000. Two years previously it was full house after full house. Although most of the decisions made by Jimmy Armfield were wrong, I have to say that I have a lot of respect for him. He has told me since that the task he had been given was a very difficult one, and so it proved. Jimmy is a very nice man with a lot of football knowledge, but to go into a club like Leeds which had been governed with an iron fist you needed to be tough, strong and uncompromising.

One bonus for the club in this season was the re-emergence of Eddie Gray, who had been told that his playing career was over and was by now coaching the juniors. Arthur Graham was a good signing, for both the club and the drinking school, and the reason for me dropping into midfield. Hart got off to a poor start, giving away goals and scoring a couple of own goals, but he improved to become a solid, reliable player despite becoming embroiled in the prevailing laissez-faire attitude at the club.

The writing was on the wall for Jimmy. It was quite obvious that he would be replaced at the end of the season and Maurice Lindley, not for the first time, took over as caretaker manager. Maurice, a real character, had been chief scout at the club since the early Revie days. He loved horse racing and was a real punter. You would go into Maurice's office and he would be on the telephone, more likely than not tuning in to a race commentary. With anybody else he would pretend to be engrossed in fictitious conversation the moment the door opened, but if I was the one making the entrance he would just say: 'Shhh, I'm listening to this race.' To a director it would appear as though he was trying to sign a player!

Maurice was the kind of guy who, if there were ten clocks on the wall all showing six o'clock and you asked him the time, would say: 'Oh, I don't know, lad.' You'd say: 'Nice day, Maurice,' and he would reply: 'Erm, well . . .' This was the result of a sort of protective instinct, so that he could not be pulled up about anything. He never took a chance, forever sitting on the fence. And he would always carry a piece of paper about with him so that anybody who saw him would think that he was involved in official business, when really his job didn't start until after the two o'clock at Wincanton! There are a lot of people at football clubs who are always conscious that observations and comments can come back to haunt them, so they take the middle road every time. You could never say: 'Maurice told me that . . .' because the manager would know that Maurice never told anybody anything.

Probably the last person that anybody expected would replace Armfield was the great Jock Stein, who had been such a fixture at Glasgow Celtic. For Leeds to prise him out of retirement and out of Scotland was a major surprise, until it was reported that he had agreed to join purely and simply because he had got himself into gambling debts and needed the money. That was nothing to do with us. He had been a legendary manager at Celtic and for Leeds, at this time, the number one priority was a very strong leader: somebody with some presence and the ability to get the club back on its feet.

Everybody, myself included, greatly looked forward to his arrival, and if that was swift and unexpected then so, just seven weeks later, was his departure for the Scotland job without ever having signed a contract with Leeds. When Jock arrived on the scene at Elland Road I had a racehorse, and after a couple of weeks I was summoned to his office. All the lads knew I liked a bet, but the question that greeted me was surprising, to say the least. I was anticipating something serious concerning football matters but Jock said: 'Have you got any tips for today?' Here was a man whose debts had been cleared and was supposed to have stopped gambling, but we became friendly through our common interest in the Turf. Jock used to have an in with Gordon Richards' stable at Greystoke in Cumbria and I would receive bits of information from stables in Wetherby, so every morning we would compare notes.

We awaited his first team talk with some trepidation. They were notorious for their candour and Jimmy Johnstone and all the Celtic lads, we knew, were petrified of him. But at our initial meeting at the annual pre-season photocall he appeared quite mellow, with an attitude along the lines of: 'Look, I don't have to tell you players what to do. You've all done it before.' It was obvious that he did not want to fall out with anybody. He, basically, had in his own mind a plan – to come to Leeds, get himself sorted out and get off as soon as possible. Whether he knew that he would, in a short time, be the manager of Scotland, I don't know, but that would seem to have been the case. It was while serving in this capacity that Jock died of a heart attack at the age of 62, moments after watching Scotland score a late equaliser against Wales at Ninian Park to keep alive hopes of qualifying for the 1986 World Cup.

In the short period of time that he was at Elland Road he got the players back on track. A man of his reputation – in his 11 seasons at Parkhead, Celtic became the first British side to win the European Cup, they had won the league ten times, the Cup seven and the League Cup six – was bound to win the instant respect of the players, and he did.

There had been two further, significant departures. Allan Clarke, who had always harboured managerial ambitions, left in 1978 to join Barnsley as player-manager. He had been unsettled at Leeds ever since Bremner went. They were great buddies, always together even until the day Billy died. They thought a lot of each other. Whereas I, an easy-going individual, could laugh about the Armfield reign and

119

all its goings-on, Allan despised the situation and could not hide his feelings. He didn't want to play, he was sulking and complaining, and it was no surprise when he left. He was always going to grab the first chance that came along. One of the greatest strikers in the history of the English game, with a simple, effective technique, he was virtually unfathomable off the pitch. We lived close by each other and where one day he would go out of his way to offer a lift, the next you would ask for one because your own car was being serviced and he would say: 'Oh, I'm going the other way.' If he was just in that mood he could be impossible. Jimmy, it goes without saying, would have been delighted to see the back of him.

Paul Reaney went off to Bradford. I have never in all my time in football known such a calculated, organised individual. A local lad from East End Park, he had come to Leeds as a forward and Don made him into the most excellent right-back. The best example of his talent is in George Best's observation that the one player he hated being in opposition to, and could never play against, was Paul Reaney. The reason was his following to the letter of any instruction from Revie. No matter what was said to him on the pitch he would simply ignore it and get on with what he had been told in the dressing-room. If the order was to mark Best out of a game he would do it, no matter what it took. Paul was so clever. He would tread on an opponent's ankles when the ball was five yards away and the ref wouldn't see it. If he did, it would appear to be an accident. That one stud in the back of the ankle would be just enough to have an opposition player looking over his shoulder all the time.

Paul, an orphan, grew up in the bosom of a lovely family who gave him a wonderful upbringing. He always conducted himself well and possessed impeccable manners. He was a super-fit lad who rigidly looked after himself. He had to. He was not what you would call a good footballer. He was a great defender. In any successful team there is this blend of artistic players, hardmen, prolific goalscorers and solid defenders and Paul was in the latter category. He was an out-and-out marker – and brilliant at it. He had great stamina, too, and even now when you see him he's still a tremendously fit-looking guy. He was known as the Scrooge of the team. We used to joke with Paul at the end of games. We were on a crowd bonus and by the end of the 90 minutes he would already have known the attendance and calculated to the penny what the pay packet extras would be. Money was his god. He would never spend a pound foolishly, whereas I have spent hundreds of thousands in not very wise ways.

Before he went off to Bradford, their chairman, Bob Martin, whom I knew, told me of the impending deal and sought my views. I told him not to bother. The reason he planned to sign him was the hope that he would bring on the younger players at the club and be the wise old head on the field. Paul was just not that kind of player. He did his own job, pure and simple. I said: 'Bob, if you're signing Paul as a defender you couldn't get a better player. Anything else, forget it.' As chairmen usually know better than players, Bob went ahead and signed him. After two months Bob told me: 'You were right. He's playing well, and he cannot be faulted, but he's not what we wanted.'

Why ask a question if you're not going to take on board the answer? It wasn't that I was in any way trying to stop Paul from getting a move and picking up a nice few quid, it was an honest assessment.

chapter twelve

WHAT'S THE TEAM?

THE CHOICE OF MANAGER TO REPLACE JOCK STEIN WAS JIMMY ADAMSON
who, as a player, captained Burnley to the league title in 1960 and
had been in charge of the Lancashire club for a period of six years
from 1970. When he came into Elland Road from Sunderland I knew
I was in trouble, even though our players called him Howard Hughes
because none of us ever saw him. During his tenure at Sunderland
their central defender Jackie Ashurst kicked me and I did something
totally out of character in going over the top on him in retaliation.
Although there was no break, he was carried off. Sunderland were in
trouble at the time and Adamson's assistant Dave 'Mad' Merrington,
whom I used to taunt during his playing days at Burnley, made his
feelings towards me known.

Now, with Merrington assisting Adamson at Leeds, they went
round the players one by one and when they came to me Merrington
said: 'I don't bear any malice, you know.' That confirmed to me that
he had remembered the tackle and, funnily enough, I never played in
an Adamson team. He wanted me out for his own reasons but, in
fairness, it was quite obvious when he came that the club was going
to go nowhere. They were struggling like hell. He had a scout called
Dave Blakey, who came up to me on the training ground and said:

'Why don't you apologise and square things with the manager? You should be in the team.'

'Apologise?' I said. 'I have nothing to apologise for. He has come to Leeds United. I am a player here.' If he was going to carry forward something that had happened two years previously then that, as far as I was concerned, was his decision. It was obvious to me that he was cutting off his nose to spite his face. But I went there every day and trained and he became more and more infuriated by this until, one Friday when I was struggling with a calf strain, he named me in the reserve team to travel to Manchester United. The club doctor confirmed that I was not fit to play and so that evening I went into Wetherby for a couple of pints. When I got home my wife said that there had been a telephone call from Elland Road for me in which it was stated that although they knew I was unfit, the instruction was for me to travel to Old Trafford. This is the kind of thing that managers do to try to alienate an unwanted player.

When I turned up the next morning I told the physio and the training staff that although I would travel I would also be contacting the players' union about something which I viewed as nasty behaviour. I wasn't bothered about the game, never watched it and spent the entire afternoon in the boardroom, downing a few whiskies and watching the horse racing on television. I'd had a good time, finding peace away from the kids to indulge in one of my favourite hobbies, and unknown to himself Adamson had done me a big favour. When I reported to the club on the Monday morning I was sitting on the treatment table when Paul Madeley and one or two of the other injured players came in. I said to Paul: 'When Adamson comes in, say to me: "What did you do on Saturday?"' Sure enough the manager came in and while he was looking at one of the players Paul obliged with his planted question. I said: 'I had a fucking great day. They made me go with the reserves to Old Trafford and it was brilliant. I was in the directors' room and this guy kept pouring me whiskies and feeding me with sandwiches and I got engrossed in the racing on the box. Then I was straight out on Saturday night. What a day!'

Adamson stormed out of the treatment room with a face like thunder. What he thought was a punishment had been a great pleasure, and he was not a happy man. He had been using transfer mentality on me and now I was giving it back to him. The transfer policy at the club of wanting £40,000 every time a player left greatly aggrieved me. When Giles went to West Brom they wanted £40,000. When Hunter went to Bristol City they wanted £40,000. Now they wanted £40,000 for me. The effect of this was to greatly reduce any amount the individual player would get from his move, and it stank. I decided I was having none of it. Adamson rang me to say that Blackburn Rovers wanted to sign me, so I met their manager John Pickering at one of the motorway services. They made me a terrific offer, but I said that I would only go if there was no fee of £40,000 involved. When John asked why, I told him that it was a matter of principle; I disagreed with their getting £40,000 for lads who had cost them nothing and given them years of service. I felt that every penny we had had been fought for and earned.

One day we were playing Ipswich Town at Elland Road and all the players were in the lounge awaiting news of team selection. I was in the group, though I knew I would not be playing. Though the manager's car was parked, he never came into the lounge and at 2.15 p.m. there had still been no indication of our line-up. One of the lads said to Maurice Lindley: 'What's the team?'

'The boss hasn't arrived yet,' Maurice said.

'Well, his car's in the car park,' observed the player.

'Oh, he went off somewhere and he's not back yet,' said Maurice.

The requirement was for the team sheet to be in by half past two, and at 2.29 p.m. Lindley and Merrington came rushing in with a line-up that they had hurriedly thrown together. The chosen ones went off to change and when the lounge had emptied I said to Maurice: 'What's going on?'

His normally impregnable defences dropped. He said that it was in the better interest of the club that he and Merrington picked the team that day. They were worried about the manager's health in view of his lethargic state.

The lads went out and did what they had to do without ever knowing the circumstances of their presence in the team that day.

Soon afterwards 'Howard Hughes' mysteriously appeared on the training ground. He shouted me off, saying that there was somebody on the telephone from a club that wished to sign me. I took the call in his office. I had become so rude towards him because of his attitude towards me, and when I asked 'Is the £40,000 fee still involved here?' and the reply was that indeed it was, I turned to Adamson and said: 'Excuse me. Do you mind leaving the office while I have a word with these people. I'm not going to speak about my future with you here.' And this was his office! He was absolutely fuming, but he was so desperate to get rid of me that he just turned and went.

At the end of the season I was prepared to go back to Leeds for another campaign, but Toronto came in and made me an offer to go and play in Canada, where the season ran from March through to the back end of August. I knew that Adamson would be on his way in the close season and so I decided to give Canada a try and remain open-minded about my future in England. When I arrived in Canada I said that it would not be long before Leeds were skint and back in the Second Division, and in the three years that I was away they had made the big drop.

A fifth-place finish in 1978–79 wasn't a disaster, but Leeds had enjoyed a good start to the campaign under Stein. Yet what was significant here was that the last match of the season saw Liverpool visit Elland Road having wrapped up the championship nine days previously and with 66 points, one fewer than the First Division record set by Leeds a decade earlier. They won 3–0 and finished the campaign with just four defeats, none of them at Anfield, and a record low goals-against tally of just 16 in 42 matches.

The season 1979–80 saw Leeds finish 11th in the league. They didn't last long in the UEFA Cup and they fell at the first hurdle in both domestic cup competitions. What was happening at this time was that they were spending big money on average players, individuals who were not good enough to make an impact in the top flight. Adamson fell on his sword.

He was replaced by Allan Clarke and it was unfortunate that it was under his management that the club was relegated. He was unlucky. The season 1981–82 saw the introduction of three points for a win, and had it been calculated in the traditional way Leeds would not only have survived but been comfortably off in mid-table. Their trouble was that they drew too many games. By then I had linked up with John Giles at Vancouver Whitecaps, and the fall from grace of Leeds gave neither of us any pleasure. Going to Vancouver as John's assistant and player was like turning the clock back, because also in their ranks were David Harvey and Terry Yorath. We also had a young Peter Beardsley. My job in the close season was to find some likely players to take over there and Johnny had asked me to watch a Mansfield player in action in a cup game at Carlisle. He rang after the match to enquire about the lad's abilities and I told him that while he was not a bad player he would not be ideally suited to the Astroturf used in the North American league of which we were a part.

Players needed a slick, smart touch on that surface and I was able to tell Johnny: 'I've seen the best young kid I have set eyes on for years, and that includes a lot we have had at Elland Road.' His ears pricked up because he knew that I was not easily impressed. 'His name's Peter Beardsley.' John determined to have him checked out further and the Liverpool scout present was a friend of Tony Waiters, who was our general manager at Vancouver. They had a word with the Anfield representative, who reported that, in his opinion, Beardsley was an 'in-and-out' performer, but I insisted that what I had witnessed up at Carlisle was a player with great control and terrific vision.

The weather conditions made it impossible to train in Canada in the close season and three weeks after our conversation Johnny was bringing the Whitecaps over to England and Ireland to play some friendlies. We found ourselves at Bisham Abbey, and Johnny decided that he would take the opportunity to watch Beardsley in action in a match Carlisle were playing not far away at Brentford. Within two minutes of the game starting John turned to me and said: 'You're right about that kid.' Straight from the kick-off he had tried something eye-catchingly different and John had made up his mind. We signed Beardsley for £100,000.

I spent a further year in Vancouver, with Beardsley in the side, before returning to England and Leeds. Eddie Gray had replaced Clarke at the helm and by now Leeds were in Division Two and in such a desperate state financially that they were soon to be forced to sell Elland Road. They sold the ground to the council for £2.5 million. In return, the council granted the club a 125-year lease with plans to improve the stadium and associated sporting facilities. Their grand scheme included the building of a new stand, a 5,000-seater indoor stadium incorporating an athletics track, an underground car park and all-weather pitches. This deal, which wiped out the club's £1.5 million bank overdraft, made provision for the council and the supporters' club to be represented on the board and I just wondered what the hell had been going on.

Although it was nothing to do with me, I have never forgiven the club for this. I just thought at the time that in the recent past the directors had been left with £2 million in the bank and the best team in the land and now here they were having to sell the ground to get themselves out of trouble. Worse, when the ground was sold, no money was made available for players. It appeared that the directors had lost all faith in the club and were concerned about their own investments. I accept there is no justice in the world, but some of those guys who were party to the ground sale, having half given up on the club, finished up with a tidy sum. In my opinion they jerked out of it when they were most needed.

I felt very sorry for Eddie. I had also recommended Beardsley to him, but his plaintive cry was: 'How much will he cost?' When I told him £100,000 he said he had no money at all available. Clarke had been given a few quid, putting £800,000 into Peter Barnes from West Brom and also bringing in Kenny Burns, Frank Gray and Frank Worthington. He had had a real go at getting the club out of their plight, but it just didn't work. Sniffer has always said that if he had been given a bit more money he would have got them out of Division Two. I have yet to meet a manager who doesn't hold the same philosophy!

Eddie's first task as manager in 1982 was to work to orders in getting rid of all the most highly paid players. He was left with kids who had been coming through the ranks at the club while I was away and consequently I did not know them. Everybody knows them now. They were lads such as Denis Irwin, who has enjoyed such a wonderful career with Manchester United and the Republic of Ireland, Terry Phelan, another Irish international, Andy Linighan, Scott Sellars, Neil Aspin, John Sheridan and Tommy Wright. They were just starting their careers, and what Eddie lacked was an old head to put in among them. I was between seasons in Vancouver, and just to maintain my fitness levels I went to Elland Road to train. After I had been there for three weeks the news came that the American League had folded. I was out of work, but very fit, and on the way to watch a match with Jimmy Lumsden, Eddie's assistant, I said that there were some terrific kids at the club who just needed someone with experience to help out there on the pitch. I wasn't touting for a job – Eddie and Jimmy had been my closest pals at Elland Road and this was just normal chit-chat – but I wondered if Jimmy had been asked by Eddie to sound me out when he said: 'What about you?'

I was now 36, and I didn't want to put myself in a position of embarrassing myself in a city in which I had a big reputation. Nor did I want a situation to develop in which my two big friends might have to turn round to me a couple of months down the line and have to tell me that it hadn't worked. I said that I wasn't entirely happy about the prospect, but I was more comfortable with the offer of playing on a monthly contract. That was how we proceeded. I was amazed at the quality of the players under Eddie, but I was the only one with experience. Despite there being no other new faces we finished tenth in the league in 1983–84 and seventh the following season. We were hotly tipped for a return to the top flight in 1985-86. Although he brought in Ian Snodin from Doncaster, Eddie wasn't given any real money to aid the cause. He was quickly labelled, not least in the boardroom, with the reputation of being too nice a lad, and not strong enough to be a manager. This was a load of rubbish. I had worked for a lot of managers and it was clear to me that he was on top of the job and in control. The club discipline was excellent. Both Eddie and Jimmy were quite capable of dishing out bollockings where they were needed, the players trained properly and they trained hard. The directors' views were, in my opinion, a cover-up for their failure to give him the financial backing that he needed.

We made a poor start to the 1985–86 campaign for which we were so strongly fancied, losing three and drawing two of our first five matches. Although we were not playing badly we just couldn't score. We did, however, turn things round and it was on the back of three wins and a draw that we went to Walsall in the League Cup on a Wednesday evening amid increasing speculation concerning Eddie's future. I was told that Keith Mincher, a member of the training staff, had travelled to the Midlands in a director's car in the belief that Leeds would get beaten, Eddie would be sacked and the door would be opened for this individual to put his name in the frame. As events transpired, we won 3–0 at Walsall. Notwithstanding this, I was greeted at training on the Friday morning by one of our great clubmen, Peter Gumby, who said: 'Eddie's gone.' Thinking he must mean 'gone' to the dentist, 'gone' to the toilet, or 'gone' to see a player, I said: 'Gone where?'

'He's gone,' Peter said. 'He's been sacked.'

Eddie had been to see the chairman, Leslie Silver, to make known his displeasure at the Judas in the camp and insisted on his removal. When it became a him-or-me situation it was clear that the chairman had been listening too readily to Mincher's representations. He fired Eddie, and this act provoked some amazing scenes. Silver's car was vandalised and fans besieged the ground with chants of 'Silver out'. Eddie had been made the scapegoat for the directors' lack of belief in Leeds United Football Club, and there was to be a sting in the tail. I was the club captain, and at a players' meeting it was unanimously agreed that there was no way anybody would play the next day if Mincher was appointed in Eddie's place. It was my job to tell this to the chairman, and when he came into the dressing-room with Mincher and Gumby and the rest of his staff his opening remark was that he was sorry that Eddie had gone. I don't think he was sorry at all. You don't sack a man and then express sorrow. They were crocodile tears.

I stood up and said: 'We don't agree with it. We think what has happened is diabolical. I have been asked to pass on a message. The players will not turn out tomorrow if he (Mincher) is in charge.'

'What do you mean?' snapped Silver.

I replied: 'We have heard that he is the reason for Eddie's sacking. As far as we are concerned, we will not play for him.'

Silver had come to announce that Mincher would be in charge of the team for that weekend and left having to revise his plans. This development had rocked him. He returned with the message that in fact Peter Gumby would assume control. Now Peter, a Leeds lad who had never really hit the heights as a player but who was a good coach, was popular with everybody. We realised, in spite of our black mood, that we would have to play the game and here was a fair compromise. The players responded to Peter and we had a fair go in the home game against Middlesbrough. It was goalless until very late in the game, when we were awarded a penalty. As I placed the ball on the spot the notion ran through my mind: 'I'm going to miss this on purpose.' I was so upset by what had happened, but I composed myself with the thought that I could not let down the 14,000 loyal fans who were there. I scored.

I had been preceded back into the Leeds ranks under Eddie by David Harvey. They do say about goalkeepers that they are a breed apart and

David was certainly that. In our time together at Vancouver he was disposed towards taking sleeping tablets on the night before a match and unfortunately he was prone to mixing them with alcohol. He would get blitzed out of his mind. At two o'clock one morning there came a knock at the door of John Giles's home, where I was staying, and standing there in a confused and dazed state was David. He was rubbing his neck and covering his eyes and when I enquired what had happened he said: 'I took the sleeping tablets and thought I was getting into bed, but I was actually getting into the car. I drove down the road and ran straight into a parked skip. I'll be all right.' I awoke John, told him David was here and that he'd had a car crash and went off to make a cup of tea. David kept assuring John that, with the help of a couple of painkillers, he would be fit to play that afternoon, but we were not so sure. John rang the doctor, who arranged to meet him and David at the hospital while, with the kick-off not long away and me playing, I went back to bed.

The following morning John told me: 'A couple of painkillers? The doctor told me that if I had braked hard on that journey he would have died. His neck was broken and hanging on by a thread.' After the game I went to the hospital with John to be confronted by Hannibal Lecter. David had this frightening contraption covering the whole of his head and neck, and was to remain in that state for many weeks. I was convinced that he would never play again and was amazed when he did.

A further insight into David's unusual personality came when I bumped into him one day after he had left Leeds. He was always doing strange things, and it came as no surprise when I asked him what he was doing with himself those days that he said he was into market gardening. 'It's wonderful,' he said. 'I'm living in a field in Pocklington, near Stamford Bridge, and in each quarter of the field I have planted flowers which represent all four seasons of the year. With the changing of each season I move my caravan into the appropriate section of the field so that I can look out onto floral displays all the year round. It's idyllic.'

David would arrive at Elland Road in a dirty, stinking old van and emerge wearing wellington boots. In the back of the van was always a massive, long-haired German shepherd dog and when it came to holiday time he would reveal that he and this dog were off together in the van to Scotland. They would sleep together in the back. 'The horse racing circuit is in full swing,' he would say, 'and it's great because I can park up on the course at Edinburgh and when we wake up I can take the dog for a good walk before the racing starts. I move around the racecourses and the nights are lovely. I get a bottle of Scotch and it's quite blissful, just me and the dog, in the back of the van.' It was a gypsy existence, really, and people would normally keep those things to themselves. But David seemed to rejoice in his chosen lifestyle. He always said that he would eventually go as far north as he could, buy a croft and read books, and he has taken to living on the remote isle of Mundy, which is three days' sailing from the northernmost point of Scotland. He literally dropped out. He's a part-time postman there, though I do wonder what weight of mail there might be in a community of 500 people. I have never been quite sure whether he's one of those super-intelligent human beings close to the edge or whether he went over the top. During my last conversation with him he said that he was going to breed dogs. When I said that, surely, Mundy could only accommodate so many canines he replied that he was going to put the puppies in his trusty old van and bring them down to England to sell. I don't think that plan ever came to fruition. He went for security with the Post Office. It takes all sorts. But David was a great goalkeeper and a lovely lad.

chapter thirteen

EARLY BATH

THE DAY THAT BILLY BREMNER WAS APPOINTED AS SUCCESSOR TO EDDIE GRAY in October 1985, I received a telephone call from a laughing John Giles. 'I see your pal Billy has got the job,' he said. 'I wouldn't bother buying any new boots if I were you!' I told John that the news of Ian Snodin's promotion to club captain ahead of me had been leaked in the *Yorkshire Evening Post*, and he wasn't far out with his estimation when he said: 'Well, you know what to expect.'

Bremner could not make his intentions more obvious by dropping me as well as making Snodin captain. After all, I had scored the winning goal in the last game. Now we had enjoyed a good first half at Barnsley, but Bremner's half-time order, 'Get in the bath, Lash,' signalled the end for me. Being a spare part at the club was embarrassing for me. All the youngsters whom I had helped to nurture were still there and they wondered: 'What's going on? We thought you two were pals.' I, too, thought we were pals, but the feeling can hardly have been reciprocal. It was quite obvious that he could not wait to get me out of the door. Whether he was under orders from the board – of course I had been a thorn in their sides during Gray's sacking – I don't know. I went weeks and weeks just hanging round the club doing nothing until eventually I went to see him. 'What's up, Billy?' I asked. 'What have I done?'

'I want you out of the club,' he said. This was a guy with whom I had played for 20 years and driven up to Scotland a hundred times, yet he didn't feel that the courtesy of an explanation was necessary. I never discussed the matter with him. If, at any time, he had called me into the office and said that it was the best thing for all parties that I went, then I would have shaken hands and said 'Fine'. But to be frozen and embarrassed out of the club was completely degrading. He plummeted in my estimation. Not as a footballer, but as a person.

Billy was an amazing guy; a Jekyll and Hyde character. You never knew where you were with him. If ever someone was going to do to John Giles what happened in the managerial stakes then Billy would be that man. In matches we'd win, say, 2–0 and have a smile on our faces. Billy, having played poorly himself, would say: 'If you're happy with that you should look at yourself in the mirror. We were crap.' He did this once too often and one day one of the lads said: 'No, Billy. We weren't crap. You were crap.' His whole focus in the game, and life itself, was Billy. Very self-centred.

Billy also had a ruthless streak. Whenever he felt that one of his signings was not working out, rather than tell the player concerned he would keep him back late in the afternoons and subject him to running endlessly round the pitch with the objective of sickening him so much that he would want to move. I don't know what he was trying to prove by doing these things. As a player I could never fault him. But some of the things he did to people on a personal basis were baffling.

He gave Armfield a torrid time. On that trip to Marbella after the European Cup final Billy and Allan Clarke had been carrying on and singing and making a lot of noise, to the extent that the manager called a meeting to say that we would be sent home if there was a repeat of the revelry. Conspicuously absent from this meeting were Bremner and Clarke, the chief culprits, and one of the lads said: 'Just a minute. Billy and Allan are not here.' Of course Jimmy, well aware that he would get plenty of stick from the pair, was more than happy to hold the meeting without their presence. He was frightened of them. Jimmy dispatched Bob English, the physio, to their rooms with the instruction that they were immediately to attend the meeting, but five minutes later he returned looking very sheepish. 'Well?' said Jimmy. 'Did you tell Billy I wanted him? Did you tell him?'

'Yes, boss, I told him,' English reluctantly said.

'Did you tell him I want him down here? Now?' said Armfield.

'Yes, I told him,' said an ashen-faced Bob.

'What did he say?'

'He says you've to go and fuck yourself, boss.'

Bob, a lovely Irish lad who had been round the club for years, was embarrassed. He didn't want to have to say in front of everybody what Billy's response had been but, of course, he had no choice.

Once Revie had left, Bremner would have been impossible for anybody to handle. And under Armfield he created a split in the camp. There was a pro-Bremner faction and an anti-Bremner faction. There were certain guys whom Billy did not like at all, and if Billy didn't like you, you knew about it.

Billy didn't give a toss about anybody, as I also discovered on the Scotland trips. He was very influential up there and his country had a succession of very weak managers with the likes of Bobby Brown and Willie Ormond. Billy controlled them, and he revelled in the situation. He ran the show.

Bremner had a fairly successful first season in charge, but one of the things that amazed me as I looked at the club's affairs from afar was his ineptitude in the transfer market. A blind man could see that all those kids brought along by Eddie Gray had big futures in the game, yet those excellent full-backs Denis Irwin and Terry Phelan were given free transfers, Irwin to Oldham and Phelan to Swansea. Andy Linighan and Tommy Wright also went to Oldham, where their manager Joe Royle was using Bremner's flawed judgement to his advantage. Royle was later to sign another of the Leeds cast-offs in Andy Ritchie, who was eventually to become the Latics manager and take the accolade in a fans' poll as the best ever player at Boundary

Park. Royle had snapped up this quartet from Leeds for the grand total of £180,000. What happened to me at the age of 38 was probably only to be expected, but I could not believe the naivety of Bremner in allowing such exciting young talents as these to slip through the net. Scott Sellars, too, went to Blackburn for £20,000 and later, under Howard Wilkinson, Oldham were again the beneficiaries when John Sheridan became another to depart. All of these escapees went on to have glittering careers. Maybe Bremner's reasoning was that the only way he could see of getting Leeds out of the Second Division was to rely upon older, more experienced players. That's fine. I can see that. But at the end of the day he would still have to bring in better players to survive and prosper among the élite. Surely, for £200,000, this sextet could have been kept at the club, who cannot have been that desperate for that kind of money.

He brought in David Rennie for £50,000, Brendan Ormsby for £65,000, Jackie Ashurst for £35,000, Bobby McDonald for £25,000 and Peter Haddock for £45,000. They were all reasonable players, but they were in the twilight of their careers and one thing they would not do would be to improve. The crowds had dwindled to below 10,000 and the rot had set in.

Now I had to think about my own future. I had offers from Blackburn and a few other clubs, but I decided that it would be nice to get out at Leeds, the club where I had started. I was still very fit and could have played at a lower level, but all in all I didn't want to feel degraded. Then, out of the blue, came an offer to go and play and coach in Israel with Hapoel Haifa. I felt it was timely and appropriate, because it was only for six months until the end of their season and would allow me the space to think about what I was going to do with the rest of my life. Events at Leeds had come as something of a shock. One minute I had been club captain, highly respected and playing well; the next I was on the scrapheap. I needed time to get away and think, and this was the perfect opportunity. The idea when I went there was to play as well as coach, but local rules dictated that players had to be Israeli nationals. One of the reasons they had got me to go over there was that the procurement of a big name might persuade the Israeli FA to relax this restriction and open up the game to foreigners.

My defection prompted some remarkable stories back in England. There was speculation that I had changed my name, my identity, and my religion and had even been circumcised in order to be more readily accepted by the local community. All of these things were real issues, however, and the club was using the line that I was very close to the big Jewish community which has always inhabited Leeds and that I had been inducted in Judaism. To this end, they sent me en route to Israel to New York, where I was to spend a week in the company of Rabbi Rabinowitz in Long Island. His task was to give me a crash course in the faith, the history and the culture so that I might feel better prepared and more comfortable when confronted with the immigration authorities and the Israeli FA.

The club had not been doing well. When I arrived they had lost their last six matches and the morale among the players was very low. Far from just doing a bit of playing and coaching, I was told that the manager had been sacked and that they wanted me to take over the club for the remainder of the season. All the players are compulsorily in the army, so training had to be done in the evenings after work. At my first meeting with them I was informed that they had not been paid by the club for six weeks, so my first problem was to confront the owner, a man commonly known as 'Mother', with this rather important issue. Hapoel is the labour club in Israel, and as well as being its head, Mother was also the union leader. 'You can't start me off at a football club in which the players, with wives and families to support, have not been paid for six weeks,' I told him. 'You've got to pay their wages up to date to rekindle their spirits.'

'I haven't paid them,' he said, 'because they have not been winning matches.' There's food for thought for some of the modern-day players in that statement, and I pointed out that the longer he went on withholding their money the less chance there was of them performing well enough to start winning. He would not entertain my argument that the players needed the smile back on their faces if they were to come up with the goods, and my solution was to arrange a friendly against a vastly inferior Third Division team. They won easily and I said to Mother: 'There you are. They've won a game.' He knew what I was doing, but at the same time this gave him the face-saving opportunity to go to the union with promises of a turnaround in fortunes. A month's wages were forthcoming.

Although we started to play well and won a few matches the situation in which I had arrived was so dire that we were unable to pull back the 15-point gap that stood between the club and safety from relegation. In spite of this, Mother was so impressed with the job I had done that he offered me a contract for a further three years.

This would have necessitated my family moving over lock, stock and barrel and, in all honesty, there appeared to be few merits in that. I asked for a fortnight to think over the offer, but I already knew the answer. One of the reasons I asked for this time, knowing the way they operated, was that I wanted the money I was owed. If I had gone away and not returned there was little doubt in my mind that I would not have been paid my dues, so I made it sound as though I was seriously interested and I received my entitlement. Although I never went back, I have some stark memories of my time there. The Israeli in his home environment is not the Israeli abroad. Over there they are living the terror all the time. All the kids are in the army and it is quite frightening, really. It's a different world. But I had a lovely mountainside apartment and a club car and any time there were social functions and house parties I was invited to them. I learned a lot about the Jewish faith. For instance, I attended the cerimonial naming of a baby and it came as something of a shock to me when the tiny lad was circumcised by the rabbi there and then. I shall never forget his piercing scream. I also attended a couple of the players' weddings. These lads lived in high-rise apartment blocks supported by stilts, creating an open area beneath the first floor. On the occasion of a wedding all the tenants would wrap giant sheets around the stilts, making a sort of giant marquee of the open ground. Food and drink were in abundance and it was all done in some style.

Another memorable event was when I decided to take the players away for a couple of days in advance of the derby match with Maccabi Haifa. This was the posh team, supported by the wealthy people in the district, and I wanted my players to go into the game with a feelgood factor. One of the personal benefits of this was that I was able to see the Golan Heights and now, when Israel is at the forefront of the international news, as so often it is, I am able to have an overview and some inside knowledge of events under discussion. Such occurrences lead me to paint a mental picture of a lifestyle in which every couple of miles of a bus journey would bring a halt to allow on board armed state police who would check the identity of the individuals. As far as the club was concerned, we never went to the same restaurant twice, and I reckoned that the same principle which applied to the withholding of money from the players was applied to the proprietors of the various eating establishments! A more benevolent summary, perhaps, would be that the eateries were run by Hapoel people given to treating their local heroes.

But it was a wonderful lifestyle. The weather was glorious, and because the players were never in before four o'clock owing to their day duties I was able to rise at leisure, go for a bagel and smoked salmon sandwich breakfast, head for the beach for a little five-a-side game with the locals I had quickly come to know and to top up my tan, do an hour and a half's training with players who were a fine bunch of lads, get showered and then out for a meal in the evening.

This could go on no longer than it did, however. I returned home to Leeds with my mind made up that I would not even entertain asking Gillian to move to Israel with the two boys, and my next venture in life was unpredictable. Ronnie Teeman, a solicitor who had done a lot of player contracts at Leeds, had just bought The Trafalgar, a sporting club in Hunslet, and he asked me to run it for him. This appeared to be a sensible, safe option and I took up the offer after telling the Israelis that I would not be returning. Regrettably, it was at this point that my personal life went a little bit off the rails. Gillian and I separated. What had happened was that we had drifted apart. I had spent three years in Canada and a short time in Israel during which the only times we were together were in the school holidays. Gillian had got into horses in a big way, in the time-consuming and very demanding sphere of teaching dressage. She had, quite rightly, made a life of her own and my reluctance to ask her to become less involved was matched by her own will to carry on. Now, at the sporting club, I was working until two or three in the morning and Gillian was rising at five to tend to the horses. Although we were living under the same roof it could never have been construed as a normal married life. There were no problems; no great rows. It was merely an existence, with no immediate signs that things might change.

Then, at the club, I met Susan. We started to go out together and it became pretty plain to Gillian that things were not as they might have been. We didn't need lawyers. Just a chat. The Trafalgar was subject to a compulsory purchase order and at this time, 1987, The Commercial public house, owned by a friend of mine, was coming up for sale. I decided to buy it and Susan, who has been my partner since then, moved in with me. Gillian and I have never had any major problems. I determined to make financial provision for the boys as best I could. There is much to enjoy in the lifestyle of a footballer but one of the negatives, probably the biggest, is that you do not see your children growing up. I saw very little of mine. Leeds' success meant that we were always travelling here, there and everywhere, so that there was very little semblance of a family life. The life of a footballer's wife, too, can be very lonely. I did not think about these things until I had finished my career but then, when I analysed my own life, I realised that there was a price to pay by your family for your own glamorous lifestyle. I should have spent more time at home than I did, but after four dry days I would be dying for a drink with the lads. I felt torn. The old cliché about going out for fish and chips and returning at 4 a.m. applied several times and yes, there are things that I regret. But I am not the kind of guy who is comfortable just sitting around, cloaked in domesticity. I like to be on the move. My overview is that I did my best for my family. Gillian is a lovely girl with a lovely family and I am lucky enough now to be with another lovely girl also with a lovely family. I have been lucky in that way, but maybe they feel otherwise, having been landed with me! I am selfish. The way I look at things is that I only have one life, and I am going to live it the way I want to. I have probably done that without consideration and respect for the people around me. But I have never done it with any malice. If ever I was in social circumstances in which I was enjoying myself I would never ring home. Why get two bollockings? You're going to get one when you get home anyway.

Billy died before I ever had the chance to ask him the real reason for my dismissal. Only a couple of days before he passed away he came into The Commercial and was laughing and joking as usual. He was that kind of guy. It was as though he expected you to forgive and forget the indignity he had heaped upon you. He'd say 'Lash this' and 'Lash that', coming over as your best mate when not long previously he'd stuffed you. The man was an enigma.

chapter fourteen

HOWARD'S WAY

MANAGERIALLY, BILLY BREMNER WAS A LITTLE UNLUCKY. IN 1987 HE GOT
Leeds to the semi-finals of the FA Cup against Coventry, who beat
them on their way to winning the trophy. He also steered them to a
place in the play-offs, losing out on promotion to the First Division
to Charlton. The home leg against the London club provided an
incident which I have neither forgotten nor forgiven. My elder son,
Simon, who always went along to watch me play and continued to
support Leeds, rang to ask if I could get two tickets for this game.
When I called the club secretary, told him who I was and asked if I
could have the tickets, he said that there would be no problem. We
looked forward to the game, but when I returned from doing some
errands I was told that Leeds had rung with the message that,
although I could have the tickets, I would have to pay for them. After
23 years' service, and never previously having made such a request, I
thought that was a fine way to carry on. On principle, I refused to go
to the game. However, I went to the ground, paid for the tickets and
left them in an envelope for Simon to collect, having told him that
something had come up, I was unable to go and that he should take
along a friend instead.

The message filtered back to me that Bremner had heard that some of the ex-players going to matches had been having a dig at the club, although my informant was at pains to point out that I did not figure among these. Bremner's instruction was that all former players should now be made to pay if they wished to see a game, and this was the beginning of an era in which all former representatives were made to feel unwelcome guests at the club, not just by the manager but also by board members like Leslie Silver and Bill Fotherby. I went to see Silver, the chairman, because the club has an ex-players' association which had the miserly allocation of just four match tickets when many more were desired. Sympathetic though he was, there was no increase.

Bremner was dismissed in 1988 and replaced by the former Sheffield Wednesday manager Howard Wilkinson who, although doing many great things for the club, also upset many of the ex-players. It was at his instigation that the many pictures which served as a pictorial history of the glory years at Elland Road were stripped from all the walls, reasoning that it was too big a burden for the current crop of players to carry to be constantly reminded of past successes. This, in my view, was not only a mistake but also a grave insult. Through the ages, people have gone to Old Trafford, Anfield, White Hart Lane and the like and been able to relive some wonderful memories through a plethora of memorabilia. They are great clubs and proud of it. At Elland Road there was nothing other than a big carpet with years of history swept under it and, coincidentally, at the end of Howard's first season in charge, Don Revie died at the age of 61 after suffering for two years from the incurable motor neurone disease. I am sure Don would have liked one of the ex-players to have got Leeds, who had successively tried Clarke, Gray and Bremner, back into the First Division, but they hadn't made it. It was a crying shame to see this great man, who had realised his ambition of retiring to Scotland, being ferried about in a wheelchair. He had wanted to spend his retirement playing golf, but no sooner had he gone north of the border than he was struck down by this terrible illness.

I have to say that Howard was always very pleasant, ensuring that those with former attachments to the club were looked after on their visits. And he was successful, bringing the club first promotion, then in 1991–92 the championship of the First Division in the last season before it became known as the Premiership. He was also responsible for the concept, structure, building and development of the Leeds United Academy at Thorp Arch, near Wetherby, and I would venture to suggest that he is probably the best individual in the country where matters of progress within the game are concerned. Newly in charge of Leeds, he brought in better quality players such as Gordon Strachan, Mel Sterland, Tony Dorigo, Chris Fairclough and Lee Chapman and his signing of Vinnie Jones was inspired. Whatever your views on Vinnie as a player, there is something about this guy when you meet him. There's an aura about him. I can easily understand how he has done so well in the sphere of acting; how he would win over the movie moguls. What you saw was what you got with this big, raw-boned guy, and what you got was a gritted-teeth, fist-clenched 'Come on lads – up and at 'em!'. Vinnie in full flow was not the most graceful sight in the world, but the crowd loved him. When you watched him play you thought 'Oh God', in the expectation of broken limbs everywhere, but he became such a vital member of the team in terms of his drive and his passion. Leeds also had good young players coming through the ranks in David Batty and Gary Speed, and I thought that the signing of Strachan from Manchester United to bring them on was a masterstroke. He did for Leeds what John Giles had done years previously, becoming the brains of the on-field operation.

What quite stunned me was the Leeds supporters' views on Lee Chapman, who scored 30 goals one season, 20 the next and still provoked the view: 'Next season, when we get rid of that Lee Chapman and get a proper centre-forward . . .' Big, strong and often quite lethal in front of goal, he was never really replaced. Having joined from Nottingham Forest in January 1990, he scored on his début against Blackburn and just carried on scoring, bagging 81 goals in 177 appearances before departing for Portsmouth. But the influx of top players continued with Gary McAllister and Rod Wallace and the squad was of such quality in the 1991–92 season that they won the title. Everybody said that it was not so much a case of Leeds winning it as Manchester United throwing it away, but it's the old story. The title is won by the club with most points on the board after the last ball has been kicked. It was the club's first title for 18 years and there appeared to be no reason why they should not now sweep all before them. Incredibly, they spent the following season in a relegation dogfight, which might take some explaining. I have since spoken to many of the players, and the consensus of opinion is that while Howard was good at identifying the right players to bring into a club in the right circumstances and at the right time, one of his failings was that he was unable to handle top players in the hurly-burly of the top flight. This was apparent at the time. They were just not playing at all. What was happening was that they were totally pissed off by the dull routines in training; the throw-ins, the free kicks and the corners. It was repetitive and boring. They didn't want to be doing on the training ground things they could do with their eyes shut.

As a manager, once you lose your players you are in trouble, and although they survived that relegation scare by the skin of their teeth and did quite well over the next couple of seasons, I firmly believe that if they had not replaced Howard with George Graham in 1996 they would have gone down. Typical of the lacklustre performances was the 1996 Coca-Cola Cup final against Aston Villa at Wembley. This was the first time I had ever been to a cup final as a non-player and it was a real eye-opener for me being among the crowd. As a player, you are always aware of the crowd, the support and the noise, but what you are not familiar with is the raw emotion. The lead-up time to the occasion was wonderful; the trip down to London, the high expectancy, the overnight stay in a hotel, the crackling atmosphere and all the other ingredients of a big day for a supporter. Within ten minutes of the kick-off, with Leeds getting a real chasing, all the dreams had evaporated and there were many tears. Leeds were to lose the game 3–0 and, in all honesty, it was a total embarrassment. For the first time, I was witness to just how much the game means to the fans. I became acutely aware that this was their lives. Grown men crying over a football match probably takes some understanding for non-interested parties, but there was no doubting the hurt they were feeling. Because the game was so bad, I found myself looking all around me from one face in the crowd to the next. They all wore a common expression of grief, and they were to vent their feelings against Wilkinson.

Probably the biggest talking point of Howard's entire eight-year reign was the sale of Eric Cantona to Manchester United. Scurrilous and scandalous rumours swept the city of Leeds when the transfer came about, but the real reason for his departure over the Pennines was Howard's propensity for substituting him during games. Cantona's attitude was that he should never be taken off no matter how badly he was playing, and it has to be said that although he performed well in the league he never put his best foot forward for Leeds in European competition. The stand-off between player and manager reached its climax in the first round of the European Cup against Stuttgart. Wilkinson could not wait to get rid of him, but the fee of just over £1 million raised eyebrows throughout the country. I always remember Alex Ferguson saying on completion of the deal that he would never take Cantona off, no matter what, but what killed Leeds fans, of course, was that a player they had taken to their hearts should be transferred so cheaply to the old enemy. In fact the egotistical Frenchman, who had left Nimes to go on trial at Sheffield Wednesday and had been seen by Wilkinson only on video, played just 18 games for Leeds, yet managed in that time to achieve cult status among the fans. His first goal for the club, in a 2–0 defeat of Luton, was greeted as though it was the winner in a European final.

More far-reaching in consequence as a signing was David O'Leary from Arsenal, brought in by Wilkinson at a reduced fee because of the many years of service he had given to the London club. He played only ten games before injury finished his career, and it seemed as though that would be the last the club heard of him. He went off to be groomed for a future in the media but, as things turned out, he was to return along with his old mentor from the Gunners, George Graham. When George first took over the reins from Howard the football was truly awful. In 38 games Leeds scored just 28 goals and conceded 38, and that gives a pretty clear picture of the mind-numbing austerity of the Elland Road experience at that time. It was, however, borne of necessity. Survival is a pretty strong instinct. The first thing George said when he came in was that he had a job to do, and he achieved it with a finishing position of 11th. Having done that, the transformation the following season was remarkable. Lots of things have been written and said about George Graham, but have no doubt whatsoever that his managerial record is terrific. At that time Leeds needed somebody to lift spirits and instil discipline and the choice of Graham was wise. They had just won the Youth Cup with players who have gone on to become household names, such as Kewell and Woodgate, and it was a pity for Howard that he lost his job just as his work with the youngsters was beginning to bear fruit. Such is the cruel world that is football. In the final analysis it is how the first team is performing, not what is happening in the background, which matters to the fans and the board of directors.

I like Howard. An educated man, he probably found his right niche with his appointment as FA Technical Director, as evidenced by the recent upturn in the fortunes of the England Under-21 set-up. His exit from Leeds came amid a £35 million takeover of the club by the London-based media group Caspian, whose first act on completion of business was to restore to the Elland Road walls all the pictures and memorabilia which had been left to rot in a cupboard under the stands.

chapter fifteen

CURFEW

I AM PROUD OF MY RECORD OF BEING THE ONLY PERSON EVER TO REPRESENT
Scotland at every level – schoolboy, youth, amateur, Under-23 and
full international – and it is satisfying to know that I am likely to
remain unique in that way. The key to that statement is that while
other players have honours at four levels, the amateur element
remains elusive. My opportunity came on that trip to Kenya just
before my 17th birthday when, although I was at Leeds United and
being paid, I was still officially an amateur, having not so far signed
professional forms. The payments in those days were under the
counter.

Bobby Brown gave me my first call-up to the full Scotland squad
in 1969. A former Scottish international goalkeeper who had
previously managed St Johnstone, Bobby, who had once been a
schoolteacher, was a hell of a nice guy but a very weak manager. The
match in question was a friendly international against Austria in
Vienna and when I reported for duty I did so with stars in my eyes,
for I was now rubbing shoulders with such luminaries as Denis Law,
Jim Baxter, Paddy Crerand, Alex Hamilton, Charlie Cooke and Alan
Gilzean. I don't know whether players nowadays get the same kick
from being picked to represent their countries but then to be chosen

among giants of the game who, only four years previously, I had been watching from the terraces, was truly an honour. It was also an eye-opener, because the discipline, or lack of it, was laughable. Bobby had no control over the players whatsoever. He would say one thing and the players would do precisely the opposite. Card games would go on all night as, indeed, they did right through my Scotland career with the exception of the period when Tommy Docherty was in charge. Such was the revelry that Hamilton, believing that money was for burning, would take a £5 note out of his pocket and set fire to it.

My first indication that there was some disquiet in the game about international fixtures came when Bobby summoned Billy Bremner ahead of that trip to Austria and told him that Don Revie had been on the telephone with a warning that if his players continued to return from Scotland matches in the dishevelled, bedraggled state that only two or three days on the batter could produce then he would no longer sanction their release for international duty. He told Billy that this was a serious situation and that he, along with the rest of the players, would be allowed a couple of drinks after the game but that he would be imposing an 11 p.m. curfew. Billy laughed: 'Don't be stupid,' he said. 'The lads are entitled to a drink.' My Leeds captain bartered until he had got an extension to 2 a.m., and the condition was that the manager would accompany us right through on the team bus so that he could keep an eye on proceedings. The Vienna bars could hardly have been described as sophisticated. They were drinking dens which were frequented by prostitutes, and on the walk between bars I saw two of the lads enjoying a bit of banter with two ladies of the night. They weren't trying to pull them, just having some fun. As Bobby approached, the lads said jokingly: 'They won't go with us, boss.' And Bobby, the Scotland manager, said to the girls in hot pants: 'Why won't you go with the lads? They're nice boys!' Surreal!

The young ones and the debutants in the party, such as myself and Colin Stein, were back on the bus right on time at 2 a.m. – but there was no sign of the senior players like Bremner, Gilzean and big Billy McNeill. At 2.45, the six lads sitting on the bus were very fidgety and we began to protest that we could be waiting all night for the rest and that we should make a move. Bobby, wanting to demonstrate his authority, said: 'Come on, driver. They're right. Let's go.' But he was swift to agree when one of the lads said that it would be unfair to go without them. He didn't really want to leave them behind, for these were the big hitters who, he knew, would cause mayhem if they were left stranded. But at 3 a.m., with no sign of them, we left for the castle in which we were staying. As Bobby headed for bed he pulled his right-hand man Tom McNiven, who was the physio at Hibernian, and told him: 'Right, Tam, I want you to stay up. And when they come back, tell 'em I'm nae pleased.' This was a complete joke. Of course Bobby didn't have the bottle to do this himself but Tom, too, was frightened to death. He was only on small money at Hibernian and he badly needed this job with its juicy match fee. Tom duly delivered the boss's message as the boys wandered back at various times in various conditions, but the reaction was predictable. 'Tell him he can go and bollocks. We don't give a fuck what he thinks.'

A portent for what might happen later had come at the post-match reception which always followed international games. Nowadays they all jump on aeroplanes and go straight home, but then the teams and the officials would attend a dinner function at which presents were exchanged. The lads hated this formality. The Scottish FA secretary was Willie Allen, the hardest, meanest man you could ever meet and the perfect identikit for the position he filled. His nickname among the lads was Pickwick. His accountancy was down to the last penny and he was an unsmiling, miserable old pillock who would be perfectly at home among all the selectors. At these banquets you would have 15 players, but there would be 50 selectors representing places such as the Orkney Islands and all the other small areas which make up the country. It was freebie time for them. Now, in Vienna, the head of their FA got up to give a speech which was delivered in German and relayed to us via an interpreter. The response was to be given by Allen and it was announced, to the lads' astonishment, that it would be made in German. 'Bloody hell,' said one of the lads.

'Pickwick can speak German!' Now Alan Gilzean was a hilarious guy, and he hatched a plan designed to put Pickwick off his stroke. As our representative got up to speak, Gilzean sprang to his feet, jumped on the table and raced the whole way round the room along table-tops which had been only half-cleared.

The previous night had seen McNiven reduced to tears. As card games, which involved mountains of cash, went on long into the night he had made three or four unsuccessful attempts to break up the schools, with his pleas that there was a match to be played not only falling on deaf ears but also provoking a feeling of resentment. As the tears began to roll down his cheeks I thought that the lads would take pity on him and fall into line, but there was no remorse. 'For fuck's sake, Tom, grow up,' was the reaction as he pleaded how desperately he needed this job. This was the wrong company in which to play the sympathy card. There were no hard feelings against him. He was a nice guy. But as I discovered on this, my first international experience, discipline existed only in the rule books.

I got 20 minutes in the game, coming on as a second-half substitute, and that could have been my sole contribution to Scottish international football. This match was played towards the back end of the season, and I had arranged to go to South Africa for six weeks of the summer of '69 on a coaching/playing holiday. Along with Manchester City's Francis Lee, I went as a guest player for Frank Lord's Cape Town City while John Giles played for Budgie Byrne's Durban United. When I signed up for this I had not realised that I would figure in any Scotland squad. My country had organised a tour which ran parallel, but there was no way that I could get out of the contract to which I was already committed. I was in a real dilemma. I went to see Don Revie and he said: 'Don't worry about it. I will ring the Scottish FA and tell them that you have picked up a bit of an injury and I would rather that you did not go on their tour.' He did that, and off I went to South Africa thinking that everything would be all right. But it's a small world, and when the Scottish FA learned of my journey they were incandescent. Political opposition to South

Africa's apartheid laws produced boycotts and created problems for those who went there and I knew I was in trouble when I rang my mother from Cape Town. She revealed that I had been banned for life from playing for Scotland and that the media had given me a real slating. What had also happened while I was out there was that Gillian had given birth to our first son, so all in all, after two weeks of the trip, I was feeling pretty low about not being around to see the baby and also being in hot water football-wise. It was winter in Cape Town, pissing with rain and freezing cold, and when I phoned Giles he said: 'Jump on a plane and come up to Durban. The weather's beautiful.' Cape Town were playing matches along that coast anyway, so it was comforting in these circumstances at least to be with an old mate.

I returned to a load of aggravation with Scotland. At that time the Anglos were hated anyway. Scotland had this view that every time the country was beaten in an international fixture it was because the Anglos did not have the right attitude. When they won, it was all down to the Scottish-based players. It even got to the stage where they decided ahead of one game upon a course of selecting only those players who were with clubs north of the border. Predictably, this backfired and they lost. But it was not difficult for them to issue bans in this climate. The fact of the matter was that players had to go to England to further their careers and, of course, they did. In their droves. This was a time when Scotland was producing players of the highest calibre and, like now, there were only two or three teams worth playing for. The list of players who headed south is endless, but names which spring readily to mind are Paddy Crerand, Billy Bremner, Charlie Cooke, Kenny Dalglish and Willie Morgan. The production of players was like shelling peas. There were good Scottish players everywhere. I only won 21 caps for Scotland, but as my international career included a lengthy spell in which I was banned I like to think that, in normal circumstances, I would have chalked up many more. The competition for my position alone was Willie Henderson, Jimmy Johnstone, Tommy Hutchison, Tony Green and Willie Morgan. To be picked ahead of any of these was a major achievement, and this provokes the thought of what has happened to Scottish football. Who knows why the production line clattered to a halt? These were not just ordinary players. They were stars. Every successful team in England was brimful of Scottish talent, with Liverpool having Ian St John, Willie Stevenson and Ron Yeats; Leeds parading Bremner, Gray, Harvey, McQueen, Jordan and myself; Manchester United fielding Law, Morgan and Crerand; Tottenham Gilzean, Brown and White and Arsenal Joe Baker and Frank McLintock.

Don phoned the Scottish FA to tell them that although I had played in a couple of games in South Africa they had only been easy, friendly kickabouts, far removed from international standards. But they would have none of it. Their view was that I had turned my back on them, but the simple truth was that I could not get out of the South Africa contract. Lord had sold tickets for matches on the back of my going over there, and everything was watertight.

When the qualification games for the 1974 World Cup began in 1972, Bobby Brown had been relieved of his job and he was replaced by Tommy Docherty. This was a great move. One of the Doc's great strengths was his discipline. He was a tough man who had managed such a great Chelsea side filled with players who were dazzled by the King's Road lights but whose numbers Tommy had. He knew what unchecked players were capable of getting up to. He obviously rated me highly as a player, because he went to the Scottish FA with the message that my ban was ridiculous, and that if he was expected to qualify for the World Cup then he needed all his best players to be available. To my great relief, the ban was lifted in time for the Home International championships, which were to be Tommy's first chance to have a close look at us. The structure of this end-of-season tournament was that England, Scotland, Wales and Ireland would all play each other in the space of a week, which made for a very hectic schedule. We gathered, as usual, at the Queen's Hotel at Largs, with its cold baths and sterile atmosphere, and in the players' minds the

LEEDS AND SCOTLAND HERO

only reason that we were really there was the prospect of playing the auld enemy. Never mind domestic trophies, FA Cup finals and the like, a Scot looks forward to crossing swords with England like nothing else. The banks upon banks of supporters at Hampden, the pipes playing 'Scotland The Brave', the wall of noise as you came out and the knowledge that the game was being broadcast around the world to all those exiled Scots in far-flung places. This was magical.

Having waited so long to get back into the fold, I was very nearly ejected again on my comeback. It was traditional on the eve of games that all the players would go to the cinema, having enjoyed just a couple of drinks, no more, on the way. In a corner of the pub in Largs I was in a group of six people including Jimmy Johnstone. Just as little Jimmy had arrived at the bar to buy a round of drinks we looked up at the glass panel in the door to see a pair of eyes monitoring what was going on. The steely, disapproving eyes belonged to the Doc, and nervous laughter broke out spontaneously among our group. There had been a lot of joking among the lads about how we would have to tread carefully and now we had been followed by the manager. Jimmy turned towards us, asking what we wanted, and we gestured that he should lay low for a few moments until prying eyes were no longer in evidence. But with all the noise and the confusion of the situation he could not get our meaning and, right on cue, the Doc, who had with him his teetotal number two Ronnie McKenzie, went up behind him and tapped him on the shoulder. Jimmy, a terrific little character who was always in trouble, had the quickest wit of any player I have ever known. He often needed it and now, instead of just admitting to a fair cop, he said as quick as a flash: 'Oh, hello there, Tommy. What are you having?' Tommy, of course, said: 'What am I having? I'm having nothing. You're having nothing. Get the fuck out of here.'

The picture house was cancelled. Tommy, who had experienced trouble with one or two of the Chelsea players and had once sent the entire squad home from a trip, was in no mood to be tangled with and I thought, 'Oh no, here comes trouble.' He gathered us at the hotel and informed us that this little tradition would be discarded forthwith. We would be allowed drinks after games, but there would be no indulgence before them. In fact, Tommy loved the crack with the players and really enjoyed being among them in social circumstances after games, but here he was making the point that any indiscipline would simply not be tolerated. This had not been evident in the Scottish camp for years and years, and it was clear that attitudes would have to change. They did so sufficiently for Scotland to qualify for the World Cup, albeit in circumstances which saw the Doc taking up an offer halfway through the qualifying campaign to manage Manchester United and being replaced by Willie Ormond. It was obviously a great honour for Tommy to manage Scotland, but he had received an offer which he simply could not refuse both financially and professionally. Moreover, he had left us in a position in which we were a certainty to qualify. I had been sent off for a pushing incident in one of the matches against Denmark and this meant that I was suspended for the qualifier which mattered most against Czechoslovakia.

This was at Hampden in September 1973, when in front of a 100,000 crowd the Leeds striker Joe Jordan became the hero as, within six minutes of replacing Kenny Dalglish, he headed the 70th-minute winner from Willie Morgan's cross. The 2–1 victory meant that we had qualified no matter what the outcome of our return against the Czechs and the whole of Scotland went wild. Personally, I had gone a bit too wild. I travelled up from Leeds in my car with a few of the lads and when we got back to my vehicle after the game I discovered that I had lost my keys, clearly when I had jumped in celebration of Jordan's goal. We went back into the stadium, but despite a minute search we could not find them and we headed into Glasgow, from where we got a taxi all the way back to Yorkshire. The only vehicle in which we could all be accommodated was the firm's funeral car, and there was something quite bizarre about travelling in this mode of transport while in such celebratory mood.

chapter sixteen

WORLD CUP 1974

WILLIE ORMOND, SUCH A GOOD PLAYER IN THAT FAMOUS FIVE FORWARD LINE boasted by Hibernian, was an absolute gentleman whose single flaw was his drink problem. It was probably no coincidence that Ronnie McKenzie should forsake his abstinence to the extent that he, too, began to suffer from the same malaise. The potential for farce was great, but Willie was taking over a squad which was so good, and he was such a nice guy, that, in the beginning, they gave him a certain amount of respect and refrained from taking liberties. This was such a vital time for Scottish football. Going to West Germany for the greatest competition in the game was a monumental event, given that it was only the third time that Scotland had qualified.

I honestly believe that we went there with the finest Scottish squad ever assembled. Before that, however, there was some fun on the way. We were to play Belgium and Norway en route, and on the flight from Brussels to Oslo, Willie misguidedly said to the lads that they could have a 'wee drink'. The Scottish lads didn't have a wee drink. Permission for the sniff of a barmaid's apron was, to their minds, tantamount to carte blanche for a piss-up and the boys, already half-cut from the night before, really got tucked into it. They were flying when they got *off* the plane. As usual, the accommodation arranged for us left something to be desired and in Oslo we were to stay in dormitories at the university campus. On seeing the grey, miserable place in which we were to spend the next couple of days, the lads decided it might be a good idea to get out the duty-free booze and continue the party. The lay-out of the accommodation was such that there were sets of two bedrooms separated by a lounge. I was with Billy Bremner. Now much as I liked a drink, I had had enough. I pretended to the lads that I was going out for a long walk, but in fact I went into my room and locked the door. The party started and the noise got louder and louder until the FA sent up Willie to deliver the message that there was a match the following day, a World Cup was on the horizon and the revelry had better stop.

Willie had had a few drinks himself. What nobody realised was that I was listening to the chat from behind my locked bedroom door and what I heard was Bremner saying to the manager: 'Oh, come in, wee man.'

'Right, lads,' said Willie. 'You've had a bloody good drink now. I've been sent up to tell you that this is where the party ends.'

'Oh, come on,' said Billy. 'We're enjoying ourselves.'

Willie relented. 'Okay,' he said. 'Just a couple of drinks with Ronnie and me and then we call it a day.'

Within an hour little Willie, on his gin and tonics, was as pissed as his players and was by now in agreement with the popular opinion that all the selectors could go and fuck themselves. Someone struck up the opening line of a popular song and, with the duty-free in full flow, a right old sing-song began. Things had begun to freewheel out of hand, and the drinking did not stop until every last bottle had been drained. The dawning of the next morning, with hangovers raging and the SFA officials apoplectic, was not something to savour and, inevitably, there was a summons to appear before the blazers. Jimmy Johnstone had been in plenty of trouble before, both with Celtic and Scotland. He was a great lad and no harm to anybody, but he was one of those unlucky people who seemed to get caught every time he put a foot wrong. He'd have made a rotten burglar. Once, after we had all been out for a drink in Largs during Home Internationals week, we were all flying and Jimmy jumped into a rowing boat which had been left on the beach. Darkness had fallen as Jimmy stood up in the boat and began waving one of the oars above his head as he sang 'Scot-land, Scot-land'. One of the lads gave the boat a gentle push into the water and, as he did so, Jimmy lost this oar over the side, leaving him with just the one. He hadn't gone any more than ten yards when he got caught up in a strong current, and the next thing he was way out to sea; pissed, stranded and almost totally unaided. Lifeboats, Nimrod jets and air-sea rescue helicopters waited for first light as this Scottish international footballer, who had just been out for a quiet drink with the lads, floated miles out into the Atlantic. Fortunately for Jimmy, there was a piece of tarpaulin in the boat and he was able to huddle beneath it in the deathly cold conditions. Jimmy's rescuers said that if he had jumped into the water and tried to swim back to shore he would have drowned for sure. When Jimmy walked into the Queen's, his teeth chattering and his body shaking from top to toe, Willie was walking behind him giving him a relentless bollocking and posh-speaking Mrs Ganley, who ran the hotel, said: 'Jimmy Johnstone. You should be ashamed of yourself.'

'Go and fuck yourself, you old bag,' said Jimmy.

Jimmy, Bremner and the manager were the trio the SFA wished to speak to amid rumours that we were going to be sent back to Scotland, with our World Cup bid aborted. This, of course, could never have happened, but the course determined upon by Johnstone and Bremner was that they were going home anyway in protest at the SFA's dictatorial attitude. They had, they maintained, already packed their suitcases. People never knew how close we were to going to West Germany without two of our best players, either through them being banned or through walking out, but if things were bad for them, then what about the manager? As the man in the middle of all this, he was in a right state.

There was no remorse when the players appeared before the officials, who pretty soon realised that there could have been a real scandal from which the fallout would drop right on their toes. In fact the papers back home had already got hold of the story of the impending showdown meeting, as we discovered when Jimmy's wife Agnes phoned to give him a bollocking. But when they came face to face the points made vociferously by the players were that the accommodation was appalling, there was nothing wrong in having a bonding session over a drink, the match against Norway was only a poxy friendly and the World Cup was still ten days away. The carpet was lifted and all that had gone before was swiftly brushed under its cover.

And so to West Germany, where we were to face Zaire, Brazil and Yugoslavia in Group Two. We stayed in a beautiful ski lodge right up in the mountains, playing our games in Dortmund, Frankfurt and Düsseldorf, and the security was very tight in view of the shooting incident at the Munich Olympics two years previously. We were protected by a group of crack paratroopers to whom we had to report if we wished to leave the premises, perhaps to go shopping, so that they could accompany us. The attraction of the event was huge. We had Billy Connolly, Rod Stewart and Elton John all flying out in their private jets to see our matches and spend an hour with the lads afterwards. In fact Billy Connolly, who was an up-and-coming comedian then, performed a private concert for us at Largs before we left. We got our campaign under way with a competent 2–0 defeat of Zaire in which I scored our opener with a 20-yard volley. We had reasoned that if we were to beat Zaire and then win one of our other two matches we would be safely through to the second round and we were probably unlucky in playing the African nation first, when they were really fresh and up for it. World Cup football was new to them and, certainly in their opening game, they were going to run and chase for everything until they dropped. That would not be the case afterwards, once their heads had gone down.

Next, we played out a goalless draw with the multi-talented Brazilians in a match which was unkindly described by the Liverpool manager Bill Shankly as: 'Great game? You know what that was? Two

Third Division teams trying to kick each other to death.' In fact we were very unlucky. We were all over them. It was genuinely felt by many within the competition that we were a real threat to everybody, and here we received a great ovation from the fans both during and after the game. Meanwhile, Yugoslavia were thrashing Zaire by the conservative margin of 9–0, which meant that if we were to progress we had to beat Yugoslavia in our final game. It was so tight that a draw would let Brazil in, provided they beat Zaire by more than two goals. Sure enough, Yugoslavia took the lead against us in Frankfurt with only eight minutes left, and when Hutchison, who had replaced Dalglish midway through the second half, made the equaliser for Jordan just before the end it was too late. All eyes turned to the electronic scoreboard to see how Brazil were going on in Gelsenkirchen and, sadly for us, the South Americans scored their third and decisive goal with just ten minutes left. As far as I know, we were the first team ever to be eliminated from the competition without losing a first-round match, yet this did not save us from some stinging criticism on our return home over our failure to really go to town against Zaire.

There had been another controversial issue. The sportswear firm Adidas wanted us to wear their logo through the tournament, but their estimation of the value of this advertising differed widely from ours and consequently we erased its symbols from our boots with black shoe polish. While we wanted more money and they would not come up with it, back in our hotel was a mountain of their gear, which they left behind when negotiations and relationships had broken down. So we all helped ourselves. I got back to Wetherby with half a dozen full tracksuits, which friends gratefully received!

There was also to be some light relief. In the beginning the atmosphere and the spirit in the Scottish camp was electric, but we were to be based in this hotel for six weeks and as the days went by a little frustration was creeping in. We were all fit lads, and among the cocktail of vitamins dished out to us on a daily basis was bromide, just so that our ardour might be cooled. No women were allowed in the hotel at all, and I hold up my hands to being the instigator of an incident after the Brazil game. The hotel owner and his wife were very nice people whom we got to know as friends. Besides the security men, they were the only people in the hotel, and holding conversations with them was a nice diversion from continually talking exclusively to your team-mates. Just for something to do, one or two of the lads even started learning martial arts from their protectors. On this night we were very disappointed not to have beaten Brazil, but the mood lightened when we were joined by Rod Stewart. Jimmy Johnstone did a wonderful impression of the star anyway and after they sang a duet we all joined in for a good old sing-song. The owners, meanwhile, had invited a couple who were their friends and the female half, Helga, was an absolute cracker, a real darling who looked twice as good as she was because it had been so long since we saw an attractive woman.

She was an outstanding woman in her early 30s, and we developed a plan between the lads that I would chat to her while the rest of them plied her husband with more and more drinks. She had been giving all the outward signs that she might be available, and I had been designated as the one to test the water. Her observation that she felt uncomfortably warm was promising and, being the gentleman I am, I suggested that she take my key, go up to my room and enjoy a shower. I gave the signal to the lads that they should keep her inebriated, comatose husband at the bar – he couldn't stand up anyway – and after a suitable time had elapsed I made my way upstairs. I was pretty sure she was expecting me – I had made it perfectly plain that I fancied her – and when I entered the room she was wrapped in a towel. She joined me in sitting on the bed and the act was over in the blinking of an eye. Within seconds there was such a commotion outside the room as the lads converged. It would be wrong of me to say that the whole squad had their wicked way, but not far off the mark to suggest that 80 per cent did. Thank God I was first in! It is often suggested that some women fantasise about taking on a whole team. Well, good old Helga wears the shirt. What a good sport.

The banter the following day was interesting, to say the least. What was for sure was that our spirits had been well and truly lifted.

chapter seventeen

BANNED FOR LIFE

AT GLASGOW AIRPORT THE WELCOME HOME FROM THE BANNER-WAVING FANS
was truly memorable. We had acquitted ourselves well in West
Germany and the supporters were appreciative of our efforts. Now, as
with everything in life, another chance was just around the corner in
the form of the 1976 European Championships. There were qualifiers
to be played, and one of these involved a trip to Denmark. But before
we even got to Copenhagen things in the Scottish camp had badly
deteriorated. Willie Ormond seemed to be drinking more and more
and Ronnie McKenzie was never more than a glass behind him. On
our way to Denmark Ronnie, who was acting manager at Falkirk, was
accompanied by his club chairman, who was on this trip as a vice-
chairman of the Scottish FA. On our arrival a member of the media
asked Ronnie what he thought about the appointment of the new
Falkirk manager. Nothing had been said to Ronnie by the man who
had clearly made the appointment, and this upset him so much that
he immediately embarked on a bender which would last for three
days.

I was rooming, as usual, with Billy Bremner, and at nine o'clock on
the first morning there came a knock at the door. It was Ronnie,
clearly the worse for wear and in a distressed condition. He told Billy:

'I've made a bit of a fool of myself. I've had a right go at my chairman.' Billy told him to have a wash and freshen up, promising that he would do his best to calm the situation. When we arrived for training at half past ten the manager had remained in bed, nursing a hangover, and Ronnie, rather than smartening himself up, had steamed into another river of drink and was so disoriented that when we filed onto the team bus he fell on the steps and cut his eye. Training was taken instead by the Rangers player John Greig, and on the night of the match there was the biggest cover-up operation outside MI5 in an attempt to protect Ronnie, who had simply carried on drinking all day, from himself. The Hearts player, Donald Ford, who was in the squad, was well versed in physiotherapy and he did all the strappings for the players on behalf of an incoherent and rambling Ronnie, whom we sat down in a corner and did our best to hide due to the imminent arrival in the dressing-room of the SFA hierarchy, whose practice it was to encourage the lads with phrases such as: 'You're representing Scotland. Good luck.'

Although the visits lasted only 20–30 seconds, even a glimpse of Ronnie would have incurred their wrath and the plan that we carried out was to stand en masse in front of him and jump up and down while shouting to each other: 'Come on lads. Let's get at 'em.' Fortunately, our distractions achieved their aim. Poor Ronnie. In such a short time he had gone from a nice, quiet, introverted, teetotal individual from the islands to a drunken wreck, and shortly after these championships he drove his car into a parked skip while heavily under the influence of drink and was killed.

Although we won the match in Copenhagen 1–0, there was to be further embarrassment. Staying in the same hotel as us was the Scotland Under-23 squad, which featured a trio of young lads, Willie Young, Arthur Graham and Joe Harper, from Aberdeen, who had something of a reputation for being a bit wild. I told Billy to steer clear of them in the prevailing climate, but as I sat at a table having a nice quiet drink with Tommy Hutchison, Peter Cormack and Kenny Dalglish in the lounge bar, who should I spot among the group of rowdy youngsters sitting at the bar but, to my amazement, the Scotland captain. The drinks in Scandinavia were always very expensive, and this suddenly became an issue as the bar flies sank more and more. They took it upon themselves to retrieve the duty-free drinks from their rooms and began pouring them at the bar, at which the bar manager took grave offence. Behind the bar was the most beautiful cut-glass, full-length mirror, and the threat to him was that if he did not allow them to drink from their own bottles they would hurl them into this wall decoration. At that point, sensing big trouble, my group left the room and it was not long before the police, summoned by the bar manager, arrived on the scene.

Billy and the youngsters headed off for the bright lights of the city, where they were slung out of a nightclub, and the next I knew of him was when he was delivered to the room and laid on the floor as dawn was breaking by two people whose identities remained a mystery due to the fact that, in spite of the noise, I pretended to be fast asleep. I wanted no part of this. A couple of hours later I rolled Billy over to reveal a face which was heavily swollen, though he had no clue as to how he had sustained the damage. It was subsequently revealed that he had had a forthright exchange of opinions with one of the selectors, whose final word on a point of dispute was a fist in the face of the Scotland skipper. But still the mayhem was not over. The aeroplane returning us to Glasgow featured a staircase, and Ronnie had no sooner negotiated his way to the top than he stumbled and fell the whole way down to the bottom again. When we landed, Ronnie tried to get hold of the kit skips as they moved round the baggage carousel, lost his footing and ended up going round with them. What made all of this so unpalatable was that it was done before the eyes of the selectors, and it was inevitable that when we got back there would be ructions. They were, in fact, severe and far-reaching. Billy, Joe Harper of Hibs, Pat McCluskey of Celtic and the Aberdeen pair Young and Graham were banned for life from playing for Scotland. The selectors accepted detailed reports from officials without calling on the players concerned and there was an inevitability about their hard line, particularly in Billy's case. It was a humiliation, especially for Billy, who had been a great captain and whose 54 caps were just one fewer than Denis Law's record.

The drink had got to the manager, the trainer and some of the players and it was time for wholesale changes in the Scottish camp. Willie Ormond was relieved of his duties and in came Ally MacLeod, who was to take Scotland to the 1978 World Cup in Argentina.

Quite what has happened to Scottish football in recent years, I just don't know. It is now a second-rate country on the football field, with no discernible signs of positive change. If the two major clubs, Celtic and Rangers, are not going to give youngsters a chance then there simply is not any hope. They get all the best kids in the first place, but there is so much pressure to win the league and to do well in Europe that there is room in their senior squads only for proven, multi-million-pound players. The smaller clubs are trying to give youth its fling, but they are so far behind the big two in terms of stature that playing for them is not what the kids are aspiring to. Another factor is that where many of the young Scots made it in the game only by going to England, any promising youngster is immediately tied to a contract that will keep him in Scotland for years to come. If Scotland does not get a grip of this situation all they will succeed in doing is to slip further and further down the world rankings. That would be terrible. Going back over the years they have a great record, for a country of its size, of qualifying for European Championships and World Cups, even though they never do very well when they get there.

A debate that continues to rage is whether or not Celtic and Rangers should be a part of the English Premiership. Having spoken to many of the older Scottish players, there seems to be a majority view that such a move might not be the worst thing that ever happened, in that the teams traditionally competing below would do so with a serious chance of winning the league. With Celtic and Rangers perpetually finishing first and second there has only been one European place to fight for. Their defections would open the door to three clubs, and with the rest being much of a likeness it would be a much more competitive league. The possibilities of a championship and maybe European qualification would spark interest and the crowds would start going back to the game. Everybody likes to support a winning team. As far as the big two themselves are concerned, it cannot be much of a competition in which they are sure that they have only each other to worry about. With their respective wealth and the players they can attract they would not make fools of themselves in England, but the argument goes deeper than that. One major concern, for instance, would be the travelling fans and their behaviour. There is the question over whether they should be allowed straight into the Premiership or be made to qualify for it through promotion from the First Division, and this was part of the formula of the so-called Phoenix League, a breakaway group of the richer clubs outside the Premiership which has been viewed with suspicion and doubt. I would have thought that the Premiership would want them straight in there. Full houses are guaranteed and the revenue from sponsorship would be vast.

Whatever happens on that score, I am personally convinced that before long there will be two superpower leagues involving both Britain and Europe. Football will change. I can envisage a league which will comprise Manchester United, Arsenal, Liverpool, Leeds, Celtic, Rangers, Real Madrid, Barcelona, AC Milan, Lazio, Juventus and Bayern Munich with matches played in midweek. Whether or not these teams defect from their domestic leagues to bring about such change, or whether this competition runs in tandem, remains to be seen, but what is for sure is that the Champions League is losing its credibility. Everybody knows that the smaller teams are going to get knocked out sooner rather than later and that the cream will automatically rise to the top. The effect of that is that some of these bigger European clubs are not filling their stadia for the less attractive fixtures within the competition. And the television companies are not really turned on by fixtures involving small clubs from the likes of Russia and Yugoslavia. All the big teams playing each other is a far more attractive proposition for UEFA, too, and it would come as no surprise to me if they were one day to make a ruthless decision and present it to the world of football as a fait accompli.

When the Leeds manager David O'Leary says that success is qualifying for the Champions League, that just demonstrates the way in which football club boards are thinking. They are not bothered about winning the league. The main thing for them is to get in among where the money is and that cannot, in my view, be a healthy situation. Clubs are spending mega-millions and saying at the same time, in effect, that if they finish fourth in the league then they will be satisfied. Certainly, it is a major thing to qualify for the Champions League because the fans want to see the cream of the clubs in action. In my day, to have the ambition to finish fourth would have been totally unacceptable and this is why the glitter is peeling away from the Champions League. When Manchester United played Bayern Munich in that memorable final, neither had won their domestic league. How can you be the champions of Europe when you are not the champions of your own back yard? There are really only five clubs, or a maximum of six, in England who can be permed to finish in the top four, and it is a wholly false notion to start a season with the thought that if you are one of them then you have been successful. The FA Cup and the League Cup have suffered a complete downgrading and are simply irritants to the clubs with Champions League football at the top of their agendas. The domestic cups are treated with contempt. And while everybody, deep down, will want to win the league, it is an easy get-out to settle for fourth. The fans want their clubs to win something and nobody should ever doubt, or underestimate, that fact.

In the light of all this, the sacking of O'Leary in June 2002 came as nothing of a surprise to me. Quite simply, he failed to deliver Champions League football and paid the price.

chapter eighteen

HOME SWEET HOME

MY MEDIA WORK AS A MATCH ANALYST FOR BBC RADIO FIVE LIVE AND BBC
Radio Leeds, and as a columnist for my local evening newspaper, the
Yorkshire Evening Post, has enabled me to see at first hand, and
comment upon, the progress made by Leeds United in the couple of
years that saw out the twentieth century and heralded the twenty-
first. The year 2002 marked the 40th anniversary of my association
with the club I love. Being a member of the pre-match entertainment
team at Elland Road and my involvement in the ex-players'
association has meant that, although my playing days are long behind
me, the club has been a permanent fixture in my life.

The media work has never been anything less than interesting.
When I go on the European trips which have been such a feature of
Leeds United's recent campaigns I sit back and watch the journalists
and broadcasters in action and the attitudes of the various clubs
towards them. The Spanish and Italian clubs are so aware of the
media and their requirements and by and large they do their best for
them. In England it is different. There is a prevailing anti-media
attitude, in which sarcasm plays such an unhealthy part. I learned in
America how it should be done. The American football and ice
hockey teams give total access to the media after matches, opening

their dressing-room doors for ten minutes of unrestricted player and coach interviews. Journalists can get anything they want, because the general feeling in the States is that they need the media to 'sell' the club. If newspapers, television and radio are hyping your next match then the tickets will go like hot cakes. The object of every team in America, no matter what the sport, is to get their name in the paper every day, so that people are reading about them all the time. It could be a minor item, such as an injury to a player or a human interest story concerning one of the team, but what is really being pushed is the next match. In Britain the whole media scene seems hard work for most managers. They resent giving an hour, or even ten minutes, of their time, and when they are forced to do so it is with an attitude of 'This is a chore. I don't want to be here.' You can see it written all over their faces.

Here, for some reason, the media is kept at arm's length. Managers utter tongue-in-cheek, sarcastic comments and show scant respect for their inquisitors. The Champions League dictates that they must attend post-match interviews, but even in this competition most British coaches have to be dragged into the room kicking and screaming. This amazes me. It's all right if your team is winning and successful. You will sell out. But all teams have ups and downs and eventually there will be a time when they need the media more than the media needs them. I have learned over many years how much leeway the media will give to individuals who are friendly, accommodating and fair with them. Too many football people possess a them-and-us attitude and too many managers are thoroughly duplicitous. They're all smiles if they win, but if there's been an obvious bad tackle it is amazing how often the manager 'hasn't seen it' and 'wasn't looking at the time'. The fact is that they have seen it. How much nicer it would be if they came out and decried it as diabolical. Managers protect their players too much. We have had far too many examples, and heaven knows Leeds United have had their share, of young players who are running out of control, though it is difficult to see how their unseemly behaviour can ever be completely eradicated from the game. It is no good fining today's young players. Money is simply not an issue with them, and it has reached a situation where I honestly believe that managers and coaching staffs are frightened of them. By the age of 21 many youngsters are millionaires, holding massive contracts. In my day to be out of the team with no possibility of picking up a win bonus was a dire situation. You had a wife and family to support, and a mortgage to pay, and a period on the sidelines amounted to a crisis. Now, in the Premiership, we are looking at salaries which vary between £15,000 and £85,000 a week, so the problem facing managers is how to instil discipline and how to maintain ambition and the will to win in the mega-rich people in their charge.

I sometimes wonder how I would have gone on in those circumstances. I have always liked a good time. Fortunately I kept my place in the Leeds side and kept having a good time, but I honestly feel that if I looked at my bank account and I was 25 years of age and there was £4 million sitting there then there would have to be question-marks over how tuned in I would be to my employment. In fairness to the managers, it must be difficult for them. None of them was ever privileged enough to have been in that position, so they would not know themselves how it feels. When I watch matches and observe the game in general, I often question the attitudes of some players. A larger percentage than is healthy just cruise through games, get off the pitch and go home, and it is surprising to me just how long some players are out of action through injury. They certainly don't rush to get back into action like they used to do. The game today is supposed to have the best physiotherapists available, with machinery which identifies and monitors every injury known to mankind, yet it appears that the generation of footballers of which I was a part was a much hardier bunch. Some of the leg injuries with which Billy Bremner played would have had the modern breed out for weeks. The gashes and cuts and the swollen ankles with which he emerged from matches had us convinced that he would never play the following weekend, but you would have needed to poleaxe Billy to keep him off the pitch. He wanted to be out there. He had a fabulous attitude and one which the modern-day player would have done well to inherit.

Why are they injured so badly and so often? At Leeds over the past three seasons it has been almost the norm for seven, eight or nine players to be injured at any given time and that, clearly, is unacceptable. Playing surfaces probably play some part in this. You don't get the soft pitches that we did in our day. The pitches are perfect from August right through to May, but today 'perfect' pitches have jarring surfaces. On the other hand, muscles shouldn't get so tired. There is nothing worse than slogging through mud for 90 minutes, as I and many of my generation will testify. So yes, players will get injured. But, in view of the money they are earning, are they so bothered about reducing their absence to a minimum? More likely they are saying: 'Whoa, I'm still a bit sore. I'll leave it out this week. I'll still get my 30 grand.'

One of the first trips I made with Leeds as a media representative was to Moscow during the 1999–2000 UEFA Cup campaign. We never got to the Russian capital during my playing days, so it was something I greatly looked forward to. One aspect of being a footballer is that, if you've played at the top level, you have been here, there and everywhere. But your experience of these places is knowledge of the airport, the hotel and the bus route to the stadium. You don't actually see the cities. There is no time for sightseeing, picking up on points of interest, meeting people and going out. So it is a feature of these media trips for me to be able to explore these great places on the day of the match, when some free time is available. The match against Spartak Moscow was shrouded in controversy. The prevailing temperature was minus 18 degrees, and while the Russians were insistent that the game went ahead Leeds protested, after curtailing their training session, that the pitch was too hard and the tie should be rescheduled. That would, in my day, have been a normal winter pitch. No clubs had undersoil heating and we became used to playing on hard grounds. As long as the pitch was flat, it was up to us to get some form of footwear that would be appropriate. I was reminded of the game we played in Leipzig on six inches of rolled snow, with the lines painted blue and an orange ball in use. It was like playing on ice. But we played. This match, in my view, should have gone ahead, but here was another example of the mollycoddling of players. I'm not criticising the players. Maybe some of them wanted to play. But the overriding consideration of the management would be that these players held values of £10 million and £15 million.

Moscow had its surprising elements. I couldn't believe that over the road from our hotel was a TGI Friday establishment. Here was an example of how quickly the international food chains get into these countries once they have opened up to the rest of the world. Two streets back from the main roads were scenes of abject poverty, with people who earned £25 a month trading a potato for a cabbage leaf. The Kremlin, with all its guards, was a wonderful sight, but I resisted the temptation, even in those temperatures, to buy a Russian hat. I didn't fancy myself back home in one of those and so I remained patriotic and invested in some Scottish headgear.

One of the good things about the UEFA Cup was going to the less glamorous places, such as Sofia in Bulgaria and Heerenveen in Holland, though the gloss was taken off our visit to Istanbul by the murder of two Leeds United fans on the eve of the match against Galatasaray. I was fortunate in that my former brother-in-law Tunch, who had once run the Nouveau nightclub in Leeds, was now resident in his native Turkey and treated us famously, taking Joe Jordan, Lawrie McMenemy and myself out for a meal in a fish restaurant well away from the trouble spot in Istanbul's Taxim Square. The telephone call to my BBC Radio Leeds colleague Ian Dennis informing him of the outrage put a dampener on proceedings and I have to say that how Galatasaray are still allowed to play in European competition is quite beyond me. Never in my life have I witnessed such venomous hatred for the opposition. Everything about the club, and everybody within it, is not only unwelcoming but also downright intimidating. Right from the police to the catering staff there was rudeness and awkwardness. Even getting into the stadium was made difficult. We had to fight our way in. The safety of people going there is ignored to a frightening degree and the whole of this is an unfair reflection on the people of Turkey. They are tarred with the Galatasaray brush when, in general, this isn't the case. It is the idiot minority which creates this situation. The atmosphere inside the Ali Sami Yen stadium was extremely hostile. I watched the players emerge from the tunnel under the ground at the back of the goal and they were being showered with a hail of missiles. I have played in similarly hostile atmospheres, most notably in Naples, and the question that is posed concerns whether you have the bottle to play or whether you will freeze and just want to get the hell out of it. I remember walking round the Ali Sami Yen after the game. The bus driver had arranged to pick us up at a given point because he could not park within the confines of the stadium, and I could not find it. Ten minutes had elapsed before I saw anybody from the media corps, and panic had set in by then. I had begun thinking how desperate it would be for me to be stranded in such a place. Moreover, I dare not speak to anybody in English for fear of their reaction, particularly after the reception we had been given.

Unfortunately football is one of the biggest targets for those hellbent on violence and causing disturbances. In amongst crowds of people they are able to operate while running the minimum risk of being identified by the authorities and so are drawn to the sport. Long gone are the days when rival fans would pass each other as they, like their teams, changed ends at half-time. I find it embarrassing to watch situations such as exist in matches between Leeds United and Manchester United, when the away fans are huddled into a pen. They get abused before, during and after the match and some of the scenes you see, such as charging horses, are truly frightening. Is it not the simplest thing to make it a rule that away fans are not allowed at such high-risk matches and to beam back live pictures to supporters who would otherwise have travelled? It is costing a fortune for the policing of grounds – the police probably welcome that because their guys are getting treble time or whatever – and it is ridiculous considering that only around 2,000 or so opposition fans are allowed in. As a player you like to see your fans at matches but, at the end of the day, if the players could see what was going on outside the grounds they would appreciate the reasons why they were not there if such a ban was enforced.

The season 2000–01 saw Leeds in action in the Champions League and immediately a nightmare scenario unfolded. The presence of Barcelona and AC Milan in the first phase grouping led it to be known as the 'Group of Death', which was unfortunate because the quartet was made up by the Turkish team Besiktas. This meant a return trip to Istanbul, the scene of the murder of those unfortunate supporters only months previously. Everybody thought from the outset that Leeds had no chance, and I have got to admit that inside 20 minutes of the opening game in Barcelona's Nou Camp, with United already two down, I feared the worst. I turned to Ian Dennis and said: 'This could be a cricket score.' Leeds looked totally outclassed. It ended 4–0 and only two things prevented a real, old-fashioned hiding. Rivaldo decided he would attempt a one-man show, and instead of doing the simple thing and putting the ball in the net he was back-heeling here, flicking there and generally showboating throughout. The knock-on effect was that Barcelona lost the momentum they had built right from the kick-off and, indeed, Leeds had a couple of second-half chances. My overall view, though, was that this was a step too far for the team.

They were going to need a few lucky breaks if they were going to get anywhere in the competition, and one was forthcoming in the second match against AC Milan at Elland Road. This was an encounter which had goalless draw written all over it, but Milan's Brazilian keeper Dida had other ideas. What should have been a routine catch for him from Lee Bowyer's shot in injury time changed the course of the Champions League as he spilled the ball and it wriggled into the net and suddenly, from being out of their depth,

Leeds were right on course, particularly as their next match a week later was at home to Besiktas. Here they ran riot, storming to a magnificent 6–0 victory. A goalless draw in Turkey followed by a sharing of the points with Barcelona at Elland Road left a trip to Milan to round off the first stage, and here Leeds had another lucky break when Shevchenko, one of the world's great players, hit a penalty against a post. Dominic Matteo scored with a cracking near-post header, and when Milan equalised through Serginho that suited all concerned at the San Siro. Milan wanted Leeds through to the next stage in preference to Barcelona and the 1–1 draw ensured that that was the case. Leeds had played some good stuff, but the overriding feeling throughout was one of surprise that they were in with a chance of progressing.

An element of luck was evident in the fact that they did, but fortune appeared to have deserted them when the second-phase draw grouped them with no lesser lights than Real Madrid and Lazio and the Belgian champions Anderlecht. First up were Real Madrid at Elland Road, and they proceeded to produce the finest exhibition of football I saw in the entire competition. Hierro and Raul were on the scoresheet in a 2–0 victory which had some Scottish pals I had invited down to the match, and the Leeds fans themselves, hailing this 'football as it should be played'. They gave us a hammering with their quick movement and incisive passing and there were no complaints from even dyed-in-the-wool supporters, just appreciation of the quality of the opposition. Again I felt that Leeds were playing in a league above themselves, but no such thing! They went to Lazio and stunned the Italians with a single-goal victory through a cracking goal by Alan Smith, latching on to Mark Viduka's flick and finishing clinically, beat Anderlecht 2–1 at Elland Road and then produced in the return in Brussels their most complete performance with a runaway 4–1 win. The defeat of Lazio had sent shockwaves throughout Europe and certainly gave Leeds the momentum to prove wrong those who continued to dismiss them as just a good young side.

That trio of victories was enough to see them through to quarter-final dates with Deportivo La Coruna. By now the European nights at Elland Road were legendary, with such wonderful atmospheres complementing the quality of the football. The club's ticket pricing policy encouraged families to go along and each match in its own right was like a family celebration. This was good marketing, because all those young kids who went along will become fans for life. I could not believe how bad Deportivo were in the first leg at Elland Road. They chucked it completely. A few of their players' bottles went in the face of the noise of the crowd and they rolled over, allowing Leeds to cruise to a 3–0 victory. It was a walkover. Of course, in the second leg we discovered that they had not won the previous season's Spanish championship accidentally. They shot into a two-goal lead and Leeds, in the end, were hanging on for dear life in the face of a relentless onslaught. But hold out they did, and now they were within touching distance of their first European Cup final for 26 years. Another Spanish side, Valencia, stood between them and achieving that goal and over the three hours of the two legs there was very little in it. Valencia did not have the attacking flair that had been demonstrated by the other Spanish teams Leeds had faced and it could have gone either way. They were built more on the basis of an English side in that they were strong at the back, played through midfield and showed great patience. Probably the difference between the two sides was the outstanding playmaker Gaizka Mendieta, who was terrific in both legs.

Again, the atmosphere in both games was fantastic. A goalless draw at Elland Road set up the second leg perfectly, and the dream was still alive for all-too-brief a time until Valencia found their shooting boots and ran out 3–0 winners. We could not get out of the stadium for ages after the game. Thousands of Valencia supporters packed the streets surrounding the ground in celebration of their reaching the final, with the players interacting with them on a balcony high above. It was wonderful to watch but, as always in those situations, you couldn't help thinking: 'That could have been us.' It had been a marvellous journey through Europe but, for several Leeds fans, it had been undertaken at a great cost. One friend of mine took out two mortgages to fund his travels, sticking another £10,000 on his overdraft. So many supporters – 7,000 went to Milan, for instance – will never recover financially. I know of several who missed out on the Valencia trip, taking the gamble that Leeds would reach the final and pulling in their horns for that. Because of all the money that had been spent on following Leeds many families had to forego their annual holidays and you do wonder how many marriages went to the wall in the process. One sad aspect of these adventures was that, because of the reputation of British fans abroad, the Leeds followers not only were unable to get a drink but, in some cases, were treated abysmally. This was never more evident than in Milan, where they were kept behind in the ground, and then again in the coach park, for fully two hours. They were being plain awkward, trying to incite the fans into causing trouble which, in fairness, they did not.

Leeds' march through Europe brought the inevitable comparisons between the squad which had got them to a Champions League semi-final and the Revie squad of which I was a part. My fervent hope is that they do become as good as we were. I am not one of those people who wants Leeds to be remembered for the great squad that we had. What we did was to play at the very top level for a dozen years and more, winning championships, winning cups, winning European competitions and getting to finals. We were constantly at the top in everything we did for a long, long period of time. It is very difficult in the modern game to do that because of the freedom of contracts and the movement of players. It is so much more difficult for managers. When we played it was easy for Don to keep us at Leeds because we were playing for the best team in the country. We could not go anywhere to better ourselves and, anyway, football then was not all about big signing-on fees. You made your money if you were with the best team and you won things. We were probably the top earners in England, though even this wasn't a lot. A big year for us would yield earnings of £15,000 less tax, and that was for the hard labour of upwards of 70 matches. Now, of course, many players are earning that kind of money every week win, lose or draw. To join the debate about the relative merits of the Leeds squads old and new, I think it is fair to say that the current players have some way to go before they can make such claims. For a start, they have to win something, and when they have won something they must carry on winning things. They cannot be compared with the Revie team simply because they do not compare. I hope that in ten years' time we are looking back and acclaiming them as a wonderful side, because I'm a Leeds United fan and I want to see them win everything.

Leeds will never be a Manchester United. Although Leeds are a big club, they do not have the power of Old Trafford. Debts are said to be in the region of £60–70 million and the season 2001–02 has to be a losing year through the absence of Champions League football and early exits in both domestic cup competitions. The most pertinent question concerns how long they can go on losing money. How long before the bank manager declares that enough is enough? We have already had a stark example of this, when David Batty was sold to Blackburn purely and simply because the bank insisted on deposits. Fair play to the chairman, Peter Ridsdale, who is prepared to stick his neck out. He wants the best for Leeds and has always come up with the money to fund transfer market activity. Further, he is well down the road to acquiring a new stadium, having travelled worldwide in search of corporate backers for the project. I sincerely hope that the progress made by the club in recent years can be maintained, because I would hate to see the club hitting the highway to financial disaster. That has befallen many clubs in the past.

The bulldozers are scheduled to move in on Elland Road ahead of the 2004–05 season and it will indeed be a sad occasion for me when they do so. I have seen that ground with just one stand, the scratching shed behind one goal and the cinder bank behind the other that the older fans will remember. The Lowfields Road stand was always a wreck, the pitch was a disaster – a mudheap – and the training ground next door resembled a corporation pitch on a wet Wednesday in deepest winter. At times, when I go there now, I look up at the Don Revie Stand and I still see the great man's face. I find it hard to come to terms with the fact that he and his coaching staff have all gone. You realise that you are getting older yourself and it hits you. I still see Billy down there, holding those trophies aloft, and I see the sort of street sign that Don positioned above the mirror in the dressing-room. It read: 'Keep Fighting'. I replay in my mind all those wonderful European nights, such as the one in which we were 2–0 down to Liege with ten minutes to go and won 3–2.

Elland Road was never pretty. But it was home.

chapter nineteen

THE 39 STEPS

THAT 'DIRTY LEEDS' TAG SO BELOVED BY THE CLUB'S DETRACTORS IN THE 1970s has returned to haunt the club three decades on under the managership of David O'Leary. An unenviable disciplinary record on the park, and the Crown Court trials involving the players Lee Bowyer and Jonathan Woodgate off it, have given the snipers more bullets to fire but, as was the case in my days at the club, this onslaught of criticism is unjustified. It is hardly helpful when an egotistic young upstart presenting a television show cannot refer to Leeds without the use of the prefix 'Dirty'. He is, of course, a Chelsea fan, and therein lies the explanation for the antipathy. The London media is all-powerful and it suits them to pour scorn upon a northern club while extolling the merits of those based in the south. Purely for the purposes of the education of that TV chappie, I would point out that there has never been a dirtier performance in football than that of Chelsea in the FA Cup final replay with Leeds at Old Trafford in 1970, but then I suppose that, much like today's generation of supporters which he is attempting to indoctrinate, his age disbars him from such knowledge.

The *Mirror* newspaper, having come off worst in its legal battle with Revie and Bremner all those years ago, has never forgotten that and they cashed in on their opportunity for revenge with a scathing front-page headline pertaining to Bowyer following his *acquittal* at Hull Crown Court. Their overview on Leeds concerned what kind of club was it, anyway, which erected a statue of Bremner as the proud monument to their history? 'We only carry hatchets,' ran one appalling terrace chant in the 70s, 'to bury in your head.' The *Mirror* is still singing it 30 years on and perhaps it is time they should bury their hatchets elsewhere.

We were no more physical than Chelsea or Arsenal – that's how the game was played – and a more accurate description of our approach would be 'competitive'. As I have hinted previously, when you go into any sport as a professional, whether it be in horse racing as a jockey or trainer, rugby and cricket as a player or coach, you should do for your trade everything possible to win. That is the professional attitude. The amateur philosophy is supposed to be that it is not all about winning, more the taking part that counts, yet I have watched so-called 'amateur' international rugby union in which the players stand on each other's heads and gouge opponents' eyes only to be exonerated on grounds of exuberance. Do you hear cries of 'Dirty New Zealand' or 'Dirty Australia'? No. Because they are from the other side of the world and the players have not been brought up on housing estates, such as I was, or ghettos like the Gorbals in Glasgow, as Eddie Gray was, the behaviour of these well-heeled sons of professional people is accepted. Ha-ha. It's a bit of fun maiming somebody or smashing up a hotel. Only very occasionally are such incidents written about, because it is expected of them. But should a footballer injure an opponent, or carry on in a hotel, all hell breaks loose. Double standards apply.

But if you are a pro, there should be only one thing on your mind. Winning. From the day I walked into Elland Road as a young boy Don Revie and Bobby Collins indoctrinated that winning mentality in me. Every tackle, every throw-in, every pass, every shot counts, because, as a whole, they make the difference between winning and not winning. But as the rewards of the game have increased, so has the appealing to referees and linesmen over every call. One aspect of the game which annoys fans is that when the ball goes out of play for a throw-in it is obvious most of the time who has kicked it out and which side should get the throw, yet the player who has put the ball out will inevitably raise his hands and claim the throw for his own side. The fact is that this is what players are taught to do. Ask for everything, on the basis that you will get at least some things to which you are not entitled. A facet of the modern game which annoys me intensely is the kicking of the ball out of play when an opponent is lying injured. If it is obvious that he has taken a whack and requires urgent treatment that is fine, but how many times do we see players going down as though they have been poleaxed only to be discovered to have been faking it? This will happen ten times in a game, and the great majority of these incidents come about because players are fannying. Our team would have thought: 'That's great. He's down. Let's get on the attack while he's on the deck. They're a man short.' I can assure you that there would have been no question of putting the ball out of play, and that is a pro's thinking. People might think it's only fair to wait until an opponent is back on his feet, but I'm afraid professional sport is not about being fair. It is about winning and, at the end of the season, getting the trophy.

There is, in addition, another unsavoury element of the modern game when players race up to the referee and implore him to book an opponent. This is a man's game, and if you cannot accept that somebody has tackled you and hit you hard then you shouldn't be in it. In my opinion, these attempts to get opposing players into trouble are disillusioning fans, whose view it is that the game is becoming theatrical and soft. They are beginning to question players' attitudes. To be fair, players are prevented by the ever-changing laws of the game from getting really stuck in on a match-by-match basis. All the physical players can look forward to is a succession of yellow and red cards which will keep them out of the game for long periods through suspension. When I look back on days on which I was running out to face the hardmen of the game like Chelsea's Eddie McCreadie and

Ron Harris, or Everton's Sandy Brown – who would chip a winger further than he chipped a ball – or Liverpool's Roger Byrne, I recollect an overriding thought which would be 'Fucking hell. I am going to have to be 100 per cent tuned in today. The first chance he gets he's going to let me have it.' Now, the first sign of physical contact brings a scream of protest not only for a free kick but for the perpetrator to be cautioned. I watch Leeds United's Harry Kewell in action and he is the prime example of a player who will appeal to the referee if an opponent has the audacity merely to tackle him. At the end of the day it is a professional game he is in. It is like going into a boxing ring and expecting the other guy to refrain from hitting you. He, and players like him, want 30 grand a week but they don't want a physical challenge. That is not the name of the game. Kewell is a wonderful footballer, but his constant moaning to referees, linesmen and opposition players, as well as his gesticulations, are a pain in the backside.

It was a better game in which to play in the 1970s, particularly if you were playing for Leeds United. This was because the team was so good. I didn't realise its quality – Giles spraying balls 40 yards to feet, Bremner winning the ball and distributing it economically and accurately, Hunter breaking up opposition attacks with stunning challenges, Gray waltzing past people up the left wing, Clarke and Jones scoring with stunning regularity, no quarter asked and none given – until I left the club and started to play alongside other players. Then, it became evident just how many crap footballers were earning a living from the game. In Toronto, when I went to York to keep up my fitness levels and also at Leeds, with the people who came into the club to replace the great team which was splitting up, I was given to thoughts that football was not the game I thought it was. I was blessed with having played, from the age of 15 to 32, with the best. The crème de la crème. Okay, the teams we had played against contained players who you knew were not of the same quality, but I could not believe how far below our standard so many professional players were. Everybody who saw our Leeds team, including all the old opposition players I see around the after-dinner speaking circuit and doing media work at matches, concurs with the view that we had the lot. And we were five-star entertainment into the bargain. It was like a jigsaw. The way we played football, it was always a sin to give the ball away. Revie always said that as long as you've got the ball the opposition could not score, and so it would be routine for our goalkeeper to throw the ball to a full-back, Giles or Bremner would track back for the pass then play it wide to either myself or Eddie, who would get down the line and cross for the strikers to do the rest.

The game is entertaining in its own way now. It's exciting and it's fast. But it's a lottery. I would love someone to explain the tactics involved in goalkeepers launching the ball from one penalty box to the other, with nearly every player having pushed up in the hope of getting on the end of it. Of course today the balls fly, whereas in our day it was a great goalkeeper who could clear the halfway line with a heavy ball on a wet day. Now, I don't know of any goalkeeper in the Premiership who cannot kick the ball the length of the park. The excitement in the modern game is in the swiftness of the end-to-end play, but the man I feel sorry for is the referee. He has no sooner got to where he wants to be than the ball is launched 60 yards to where he has just come from. Meanwhile, he has got to make a decision while the crowd is shouting: 'For fuck's sake, ref. Keep up with the play.' Talk about a physical impossibility. Greyhounds, maybe, but not even professional athletes could keep up with the pace of the game today. Some would say it is better now, others that it was better in my day. The fact is that if it is end-to-end stuff that you want then it is better now, but if you want to talk quality football, and quality footballers, there is no doubt in my mind that players of the calibre of John Giles, Bobby Charlton and Jim Baxter do not exist in the modern game.

Nobody, for instance, was and is fitter than that trio, and I know their fitness levels. I also know the strength of their will to win. If they were in midfield, and the ball was going over their heads as if it were a tennis match, they would have gone mad. In our side Giles, Reaney,

Madeley and Hunter would not have dared to indulge in such profligacy. They went for the short ball and were always on for it. Anything else and Don would have gone berserk. There was the famous occasion in 1972 when, in beating Southampton 7–0, we strung together a succession of 39 passes without one of their players touching the ball. Ted Bates, the Southampton manager, was Don's best friend and Don sent a message onto the field from the touchline that we were to score no more goals. That move is better remembered and more often replayed in television programmes than the seven goals scored by myself (three), Clarke (two), Charlton and Jones, but it is little known that it came about because Don wanted to save Ted from further embarrassment. Perhaps Ted had helped Don with advice through his young managerial years. We could have run up a cricket score that day against a team which included plenty of internationals such as Mick Channon, Ron Davies and Jimmy Gabriel. Unfortunately for the Saints we were on a high at the time, having beaten Manchester United 5–1 in our previous game. Name me a team capable of stringing together half a dozen passes now! Football is not played in the same way any more. And my litmus test is the crowds. When you've played in front of a full price-paying attendance of 137,000 at Hampden Park and seen, in Leeds United's UEFA Cup campaign of 2001–02, the need to reduce admission prices to fill the stadium, that is, in my view, a bold statement of the difference between soccer old and new. If the product is right then there should be no need to cut the prices. It is felt throughout Europe that ticket prices have to be dropped to attract the crowds and that, in my book, speaks for itself.

The pinnacle of the game now is to win the European Cup and go on to win the World Club Championship, yet the fact is that it can be achieved by a club which has finished third or fourth in its own domestic league. That cannot be right. We had to win the league to earn the right to be there, but it has now been made relatively easy for the top teams in England to get into the Champions League. Other than the top five teams, Manchester United, Arsenal, Leeds United,

Liverpool and Chelsea, nobody has the wealth to be able to assemble a squad which is capable of competing at that level. It's all about buying power these days, with the rich getting richer and the rest getting deeper and deeper into the mire. That is why there is perpetual talk of leagues within leagues and the Scottish giants Celtic and Rangers eventually playing a part in the English game. The crowds will be there and television wants them. The game now is not about what the fans want, but what television dictates. I have to say that Sky running the game is great from one perspective. The wives might hate it, but I can sit down at noon on a Sunday and right through until nine o'clock at night I can watch wall-to-wall football. At midday there's a live match, followed by a two o'clock pay-per-view, then the big match at four o'clock followed by the Spanish football at six o'clock and to me this is fantastic. Who, really, wants to go to the grounds to watch these matches at such inconvenient times for the family? Four o'clock on a Sunday is usually the time that the roast is being prepared, and I have to tell you that if I am not doing the radio after my pre-match corporate work at Elland Road I go home to watch it on the television. That means that I do not have to sit around in the cold, wrestle my way through crowds and get stuck in the car park. Instead, the dinner is on the table at 4.45 p.m., half-time, and I have 15 minutes to wallop it down before the second half gets under way. So television is not only running football, it's also running the nation's family lives.

Football has got to get its on-the-field product right. You can only kid people, and disillusion them, for so long. I don't think that Mr Average, earning £15,000 a year, will go on paying £40 a match to watch teams whose £30,000 a week players are not on the park week in and week out. If I am prepared to shell out that proportion of what I graft all week for, I want my team full of stars, not individuals who are out with a supposed injury which is often no more than a minor discomfort. I want to see them giving me something back through graft. I am driven mad by managers' excuses that their players are 'tired'. Recently at Leeds we had the situation where two of their players, Harry Kewell and Mark Viduka, went off to the other side of the world to play in World Cup qualifiers for Australia. They played two games in four weeks, one in Australia and one in Uruguay, and then had 48 hours to get back to Leeds for a Worthington Cup tie against Chelsea, which was a big match for the club. They were 'too tired' to play. That, frankly, is rubbish. I have seen players in the old days turn out for their clubs on a Thursday night, then be with their international squads in time for a Saturday fixture. These were players who, if there was a match, wanted to be involved. They don't now. Even for £30,000 a week. You might understand it if, after an hour, they felt tired and wanted to come off, but to plead to the manager that they would not be up to starting is unacceptable. It's amazingly tiring sitting on an aeroplane and watching a movie. I'd love to know if, when they got back after a month, the tiredness prevented them from having it off with their partners that night!

In my day, the Leeds United players were big box office. Nights out in the city after matches brought us into contact with the fans, who had paid their £4 to watch us and wanted to talk to us about football. No hassle, no aggravation – at least from the men. But it was always known throughout the game that women were readily available to football players. Being a mug for a pretty face always made me vulnerable, and although I settled down a lot in later life I have to confess to having fallen prey to the stalkers. Indeed I was probably the worst culprit for what they now call 'going off the side'. Talking of which, one of the great sins in football is that George Best was finished at the age of 25. I have known only one other footballer who could match him for natural talent – the ability to take on and beat four men and then go back and do it all again – and that was Eddie Gray. There is a body of opinion, to which I subscribe, that Eddie would have been an even better player than George had it not been for his succession of injuries. I felt sorry for George. Everybody says that Sir Matt Busby was one of the great managers and, indeed, he was. His record speaks for itself. But I can honestly say that if George had been in a Revie side he would not have encountered some of the problems which beset him at Old Trafford and he would certainly have played an awful lot longer. He would not have been allowed to get away with some of the things he did. Revie would scrutinise your girlfriends, urging you to get married after thoroughly checking out potential life partners. He was like a mafia man, picking out wives for his players. He didn't want his lads in lodgings, because it was too easy to slip into the night. What he didn't realise was that it was much easier to slip out when you were married! George was not a bad guy. He was easily led. His fame went before him and he was cajoled into ventures such as opening a nightclub and a boutique and other activities, all of which distracted him from the game. When they talk about the truly great players, and the best of all time, I'm afraid I cannot include a guy who was washed out, knackered and gone at 25. George was a weakness in the profession. They speak, too, of Cantona being one of the best, yet how can that be so when he played for such a comparatively short time? These guys, in my view, cannot be mentioned in the same breath as Bobby Charlton, who left behind Billy Wright's record of 105 England caps in the World Cup quarter-final against West Germany in 1970 and scored a record number of goals for club and country in a long, distinguished career. A thorough professional. Best was great to watch – a thorough entertainer whose individual ability was superb – but the thing about being a pro at that level is that unless you are 100 per cent fit you are not going to make it over a sustained period of time.

I played alongside and against all the greats, but if I were asked to nominate the best example of a professional I ever saw it would have to be Bobby Charlton. He had everything: a winner's attitude, the ability to go past people and an almost uncanny eye for goal. Next would be Franz Beckenbauer, who had the most wonderful football brain. There is a lot more to being a pro than ability. It means staying the course. And I am proud of the fact that, in horse racing parlance, I was a top-class stayer rather than a flashy sprinter.